Anonymus

Living English Poets

MDCCCXCIII

Anonymus

Living English Poets
MDCCCXCIII

ISBN/EAN: 9783741197918

Manufactured in Europe, USA, Canada, Australia, Japa

Cover: Foto ©Andreas Hilbeck / pixelio.de

Manufactured and distributed by brebook publishing software (www.brebook.com)

Anonymus

Living English Poets

LIVING
ENGLISH POETS

MDCCCXCIII

LONDON
KEGAN PAUL, TRENCH, TRÜBNER & CO., LTD.
MDCCCXCIII

PREFACE TO THE ORIGINAL EDITION.

THE Editors of the present selection believe themselves justified in claiming for the principle which has directed them a certain novelty, at least as far as regards living writers. They have prepared an anthology which aims at being no casual or desultory assemblage of beautiful poems, but one which presents in chronological order examples of the highest attainment, and none but the highest, of the principal Poets of our own age. So great is the wealth of English poetry in this century, so varied its field, so versatile its execution, that the difficulty has been to know how to repress and omit. In making such a selection it has been felt that it was of the highest importance to avoid anything like narrowness of aim, and above all to secure exemption from the prejudices and the partialities of any one school. The Editors believe that they have been scrupulously catholic in their views; they have not undertaken the work in haste, and they are anxious to record that, as far as they are able to learn, there is no living writer of verse, whose works have enjoyed any reputation either in a wide or narrow circle, to whom they have not given their unbiassed consideration, and that, if any names are found to be omitted here, the Editors must take upon themselves the responsibility of having felt obliged to omit them deliberately.

There are but two exceptions to the names they have wished to include. An eminent writer whose verse deserves to be no less widely read than is his prose, has declined "to be bound with others in a selection;" and while this is in one sense a great regret to the Editors, it is not wholly without its compensations, since all readers who are aware of the omission of any favourite Poet will of course consider that he, their own Apollo, is the fastidious One who has refused to allow his flowers to be twined in the general garland. The other has succeeded in

PREFACE TO ORIGINAL EDITION

forgetting the flight of time, and, being therefore unwilling that others should take note of that swift passage of years which blanches even poetic locks, is unwilling to comply with the chronological system which is an essential part of the Editors' plan.

The Editors, then, having desired to include, to the best of their judgment, representative pieces from all the verse-writers who may really be called in any high and lasting sense Poets, have been gratified to find that the names have for the most part arranged themselves by a quantitative test in an order which approximately is that in which the public voice has classed the names selected. Not, however, that the test is infallible, or without its exceptions. Moreover, it has not been thought fitting to select from Dramas, since detached passages suffer by division from their context, and hence SIR HENRY TAYLOR *is here represented by lyrics alone, of which he has written far too few.*

The present age has been particularly rich in facetious and fantastic verse, but the Editors of the present selection have only ventured to avail them-

selves of it sparingly, and where an underlying seriousness of purpose and a close attention to form seemed to give it more than an ephemeral value. Throughout it may be said that a conviction of the enduring qualities of poems and of Poets has been allowed to outweigh a mere sense of brightness or cleverness in workmanship. The Editors have been particularly struck, in reading a very large number of volumes of verse for the purpose in hand, with the excellent manner in which much is now-a-days said, which in its essence is scarcely worth the saying, and they have not considered that such pieces, though in themselves at times exquisite, are likely to be of permanent value.

It would have swelled the book beyond all reasonable limits to have included in it the masterpieces of contemporary American poetry. Literature on the other side of the Atlantic has now extended so considerably in all directions that the Americans may safely be left to prepare their own anthology.

It remains only to thank cordially all who have given permission to include their poems, and to apologise for the unavoidable prominence given to these few words of preface, the mere string which has served to tie up our sweet posy.

March, 1882.

Since these words were written, English literature is the poorer by the loss of a Poet to whom a large space had by right been assigned in the ensuing selection. DANTE GABRIEL ROSSETTI *will write no more, and although his name and fame die not, he is unhappily no longer to be classed among living Poets. It is with a sad satisfaction that the Editors mention the graceful courtesy with which he not merely acceded to their request to include several of his poems, but interested himself in their work.*

June, 1882.

PREFACE TO NEW EDITION.

*E*LEVEN *years have elapsed, and to the same hands has been entrusted the task of revising the work originally presented to the public in the words which have just been read. The labour has been a melancholy one, for the first part of it was to remove those shining names which one after another have passed, since 1882, from the roll of the living. Fourteen poets, whose work was included then, can be quoted from here no more. The first to leave us, in 1884, was the venerable "ORION" HORNE. LORD HOUGHTON followed in 1885. A fatal year was 1886, in which SIR HENRY TAYLOR, WILLIAM BARNES and R. C. TRENCH passed away. One of the youngest of the group, PHILIP BOURKE MARSTON, was relieved from much suffering in 1887. Then greater lights began to be extinguished. The death of MATTHEW ARNOLD, in 1888, was but* the prelude to that of ROBERT BROWNING in 1889. NEWMAN survived until 1890. In 1891 LORD LYTTON passed away. But 1892 was the year of pre-eminent loss, for the deaths of CORY and WOOLNER were scarcely noted in the universal mourning of an empire for the greatest poet of the century, for TENNYSON himself. One more name, that of JOHN ADDINGTON SYMONDS, has been erased from the list even while our work of revision has been in progress.

For these fourteen deceased poets, of strangely different force and value, we have endeavoured to substitute others whose work has come into prominence since this book was originally planned. Seventeen poets are represented in this edition for the first time. It cannot be pretended that among these new inheritors of renown there are as yet to be found any who fill in our hearts the place so long occupied by TENNYSON, and for not a few years before their deaths by BROWNING and ARNOLD. But it is an easy thing to depreciate the achievement of youth by comparing it with the fulfilment of long life; and it is certainly not our intention here to despair of the Republic of

Poetry. *We believe that among those poets who have secured a hearing within the last decade there are several whose voices will continue to sound more clearly and more loudly as they slowly ascend the hill of song.*

As in 1882, so now in 1893, our selection is not quite so complete as we should wish to make it. One young poet of very high promise has been prevented by health from according or refusing that permission which we are certain he would have generously given. Another writer, as did an elder confrère *in 1882, declines to be bound with others in a collection. But though we deplore these two omissions, we still hope that the book, in its revised form, may be found to be no less characteristic of the poetry of the present day than its predecessor was acknowledged to be of that of eleven years ago.*

September, 1893.

CONTENTS

	PAGE
FREDERICK TENNYSON	
THE BLACKBIRD	1
WOMEN AND CHILDREN	6
THOMAS GORDON HAKE	
THE SNAKE-CHARMER	9
AUBREY DE VERE	
SONG	15
From "ODE ON THE ASCENT OF THE ALPS"	16
LYCIUS	19
THE CAMPO SANTO AT PISA I	22
„ „ „ II	23
PHILIP JAMES BAILEY	
From "FESTUS"	24

FREDERICK LOCKER-LAMPSON

THE UNREALIZED IDEAL	26
AT HER WINDOW	27
LOULOU AND HER CAT	28

COVENTRY PATMORE

From "THE ANGEL IN THE HOUSE" I LOVE'S PERVERSITY	31
" " " " II THE REVELATION	33
THE TOYS	34
DEPARTURE	35
THE AZALEA	37

WILLIAM ALEXANDER

A VISION OF OXFORD	39

CHRISTINA GEORGINA ROSSETTI

AMOR MUNDI	44
UP-HILL	46
SONG	47
BIRD RAPTURES	48
NOBLE SISTERS	48
AT HOME	51
DREAM LAND	52

CHRISTINA GEORGINA ROSSETTI—continued

AFTER DEATH	54
From " TIME FLIES " I	55
,, ,, ,, II	55
,, ,, ,, III	57
,, ,, ,, IV	57

SIR EDWIN ARNOLD

From " THE LIGHT OF ASIA "	59
TO A PAIR OF EGYPTIAN SLIPPERS	61

LEWIS MORRIS

AT LAST	66
THE HOME ALTAR	69
From " GWEN "	71
THE BEGINNINGS OF FAITH	74
THE ODE OF DECLINE	75
ON A THRUSH SINGING IN AUTUMN	80

RICHARD WATSON DIXON

SONG	83
From " CHRIST'S COMPANY " THE HOLY MOTHER AT THE CROSS	84

CONTENTS

WILLIAM MORRIS

THE CHAPEL IN LYONESS	87
THE HAYSTACK IN THE FLOODS	92
From "THE LIFE AND DEATH OF JASON" I	99
,, ,, ,, ,, II	102
From "THE EARTHLY PARADISE"	103
From "LOVE IS ENOUGH" THE MUSIC	105
THE MESSAGE OF THE MARCH WIND	107

ALFRED AUSTIN

IN THE HEART OF THE FOREST	112
A MARCH MINSTREL	118
PRIMROSES I	120
,, II	121
,, III	123
TO ENGLAND	124

SIR ALFRED LYALL

A RAJPOOT CHIEF OF THE OLD SCHOOL MORIBUNDUS LOQITUR	126

JOHN LEICESTER WARREN, LORD DE TABLEY

CIRCE	132
TWO OLD KINGS	135

WALTER THEODORE WATTS

	PAGE
NATURA MALIGNA	136
JOHN THE PILGRIM (THE MIRAGE IN EGYPT)	137
THE FIRST KISS	138

ALGERNON CHARLES SWINBURNE

FROM "ATALANTA IN CALYDON" CHORUS	139
IN MEMORY OF WALTER SAVAGE LANDOR	141
FROM "THE GARDEN OF PROSERPINE"	144
THE SUNDEW	146
FROM PRELUDE TO "SONGS BEFORE SUNRISE"	148
FROM "MATER TRIUMPHALIS"	152
FROM "HERTHA"	155
A FORSAKEN GARDEN	158

WILFRID SCAWEN BLUNT

TO MANON COMPARING HER TO A FALCON	162
A FOREST IN BOSNIA	163
LILAC AND GOLD AND GREEN	163
FROM "IN VINCULIS"	165

AUSTIN DOBSON

A DEAD LETTER I	167
,, ,, II	169
,, ,, III	170
A GENTLEMAN OF THE OLD SCHOOL	173

CONTENTS

AUSTIN DOBSON—continued

	PAGE
A SONG OF THE THE FOUR SEASONS	178
TO AN INTRUSIVE BUTTERFLY	179
THE POET AND THE CRITICS	181
A FANCY FROM FONTENELLE	184
BEFORE SEDAN	185
THE LADIES OF ST. JAMES'S	186
"GOOD NIGHT, BABETTE!"	189
THE BALLAD OF THE ARMADA	192
IN AFTER DAYS	194

AUGUSTA WEBSTER

IF	195

HARRIET E. HAMILTON KING

FROM "THE DISCIPLES"	198
FROM "AGESILAO MILANO"	200

ROBERT WILLIAMS BUCHANAN

FROM "WHITE ROSE AND RED" DROWSIETOWN	203

WILLIAM JOHN COURTHOPE

FROM "THE PARADISE OF BIRDS" CHORUS OF HUMAN SOULS	210
CHORUS OF BIRDS	213

FREDERIC W. H. MYERS

FROM "ST. PAUL"	216
TENERIFFE	217
SIMMENTHAL	220

ROBERT BRIDGES

ELEGY ON A LADY, WHOM GRIEF FOR THE DEATH OF HER BETROTHED KILLED	222
MY SONG	225

ANDREW LANG

BALLADE OF SLEEP	227
BALLADE OF HIS CHOICE OF A SEPULCHRE	229
NATURAL THEOLOGY	230

EDMUND GOSSE

LYING IN THE GRASS	231
THE RETURN OF THE SWALLOWS	234
THE CHARCOAL-BURNER	237
TWO POINTS OF VIEW	239

WALTER HERRIES POLLOCK

A CONQUEST	241

CONTENTS

ROBERT LOUIS STEVENSON

	PAGE
THE HOUSE BEAUTIFUL	242
THE CELESTIAL SURGEON	243
THE WIND	244
"SAY NOT OF ME"	245
"SING CLEARLIER, MUSE"	246

THEOPHILE MARZIALS

SONG	247
A PASTORAL	248
SONG	249

MARGARET L. WOODS

TO THE FORGOTTEN DEAD	250

MARY DARMESTETER

TO A DRAGON-FLY	251
LE ROI EST MORT	252
RETROSPECT	253
TWILIGHT	255

ROBERT, LORD HOUGHTON

A WET SUNSET IN SOUTH AFRICA	257
A QUESTION	259

CONTENTS

NORMAN GALE
A BIRD IN THE HAND 260

KATHARINE TYNAN
GOLDEN LILIES 262
A TIRED HEART 263

HERBERT P. HORNE
AMICO SUO 266

ARTHUR SYMONS
RAIN ON THE DOWN 267
EMMY 267

RUDYARD KIPLING
MANDALAY 269
L'ENVOI 272

RICHARD LE GALLIENNE
THE WONDER-CHILD 277
AUTUMN 278
ALL SUNG 279

LIVING ENGLISH POETS

FREDERICK TENNYSON

Born 1807

THE BLACKBIRD

I

How sweet the harmonies of Afternoon!
   The Blackbird sings along the sunny breeze
His ancient song of leaves, and Summer boon;
   Rich breath of hayfields streams thro' whispering trees;
And birds of morning trim their bustling wings,
And listen fondly—while the Blackbird sings.

II

How soft the lovelight of the West reposes
   On this green valley's cheery solitude,

On the trim cottage with its screen of roses,
   On the gray belfry with its ivy hood,
And murmuring mill-race, and the wheel that flings
Its bubbling freshness—while the Blackbird sings.

III

The very dial on the village church
   Seems as 'twere dreaming in a dozy rest;
The scribbled benches underneath the porch
   Bask in the kindly welcome of the West;
But the broad casements of the old Three Kings
Blaze like a furnace—while the Blackbird sings.

IV

And there beneath the immemorial elm
   Three rosy revellers round a table sit,
And thro' gray clouds give laws unto the realm,
   Curse good and great, but worship their own wit,
And roar of fights, and fairs, and junketings,
Corn, colts, and curs—the while the Blackbird sings.

V

Before her home, in her accustom'd seat,
   The tidy Grandam spins beneath the shade
Of the old honeysuckle, at her feet
   The dreaming pug, and purring tabby laid;
To her low chair a little maiden clings,
And spells in silence—while the Blackbird sings.

VI

Sometimes the shadow of a lazy cloud
  Breathes o'er the hamlet with its gardens green,
While the far fields with sunlight overflow'd
  Like golden shores of Fairyland are seen;
Again, the sunshine on the shadow springs,
And fires the thicket where the Blackbird sings.

VII

The woods, the lawn, the peaked Manor-house,
  With its peach-cover'd walls, and rookery loud,
The trim, quaint garden alleys screen'd with boughs,
  The lion-headed gates, so grim and proud,
The mossy fountain with its murmurings,
Lie in warm sunshine—while the Blackbird sings.

VIII

The ring of silver voices, and the sheen
  Of festal garments—and my Lady streams
With her gay court across the garden green;
  Some laugh, and dance, some whisper their love-dreams;
And one calls for a little page; he strings
Her lute beside her—while the Blackbird sings.

IX

A little while—and lo! the charm is heard,
  A youth, whose life has been all Summer, steals

Forth from the noisy guests around the board,
    Creeps by her softly; at her footstool kneels;
And, when she pauses, murmurs tender things
Into her fond ear—while the Blackbird sings.

X

The smoke-wreaths from the chimneys curl up higher,
    And dizzy things of Eve begin to float
Upon the light; the breeze begins to tire;
    Half way to Sunset with a drowsy note
The ancient clock from out the valley swings;
The Grandam nods—and still the Blackbird sings.

XI

Far shouts and laughter from the farmstead peal,
    Where the great stack is piling in the sun;
Thro' narrow gates o'erladen waggons reel,
    And barking curs into the tumult run;
While the inconstant wind bears off, and brings
The merry tempest—and the Blackbird sings.

XII

On the high wold the last look of the sun
    Burns, like a beacon, over dale and stream;
The shouts have ceased, the laughter and the fun;
    The Grandam sleeps, and peaceful be her dream;
Only a hammer on an anvil rings;
The day is dying—still the Blackbird sings.

XIII

Now the good Vicar passes from his gate
   Serene, with long white hair; and in his eye
Burns the clear spirit that hath conquer'd fate,
   And felt the wings of immortality;
His heart is throng'd with great imaginings,
And tender mercies—while the Blackbird sings.

XIV

Down by the brook he bends his steps and thro'
   A lowly wicket; and at last he stands
Awful beside the bed of one who grew
   From boyhood with him—who with lifted hands,
And eyes, seems listening to far welcomings,
And sweeter music than the Blackbird sings.

XV

Two golden stars, like tokens from the Blest,
   Strike on his dim orbs from the setting sun;
His sinking hands seem pointing to the West;
   He smiles as though he said "Thy will be done":
His eyes, they see not those illuminings;
His ears, they hear not what the Blackbird sings.

WOMEN AND CHILDREN

God said, "Bring little children unto me";
   And Man is likest God, when from his heart
Truth flows in its divine simplicity,
   And love dwells in him working without art:
Children are Earth's fair flowers—the Crown of Life
   A noble Woman—and he is refill'd
With hope who turns with love unto his Wife,
   With love who turns with hope unto his Child.

II

Oh! if no faces were beheld on earth,
   But toiling Manhood, and repining Age,
No welcome eyes of Innocence and Mirth
   To look upon us kindly, who would wage
The gloomy battle for himself alone?
   Or thro' the dark of the o'erhanging cloud
Look wistfully for light? who would not groan
   Beneath his daily task, and weep aloud?

III

But little children take us by the hand,
   And gaze with trustful cheer into our eyes

Patience and Fortitude beside us stand
   In Woman's shape, and waft to Heav'n our sighs;
The Guiltless child holds back the arm of Guilt
   Upraised to strike, and woman may atone
With sinless tears for sins of man, and melt
   The damning seal when evil deeds are done.

IV

When thirsty Suffering hath drunk up our tears,
   And left the heart sere as an Autumn leaf,
From her fond eyes they fall for us; she cheers
   With songs, and lights with hope the cloud of Grief;
When our sweet Youth for ever buried lies,
   And we well nigh forget the thing we were,
Once more we meet him in the young blue eyes,
   And laugh to see his resurrection there.

V

When to the car of Vengeance and of Hate
   We yoke ill thoughts, and memories hot from Hell,
'Tis She that stays us, like relenting Fate,
   'Tis her weak arm that locks the crazing wheel;
Above the dust of conflict, and the jar,
   She lifts a little child; her voice is heard
Piercing above the thunder of the War,
   "Spare thou, that thine hereafter may be spared!"

VI

And should they go before us on that way
    That all must tread, and leave us faint with sorrow ;
Should the great light of Love forsake our day,
    Memory's bright moon bespeaks a sunbright morrow ;
Behold, the skies unfold ! broad beams descend ;
    Beneath the Gods upon the golden stair,
Amid the upward glories without end,
    At Heavengate they stand, and bid us there.

THOMAS GORDON HAKE

Born 1809

THE SNAKE-CHARMER

The forest rears on lifted arms
   A world of leaves, whence verdurous light
Shakes through the shady depths and warms
   Proud tree and stealthy parasite,
There where those cruel coils enclasp
The trunks they strangle in their grasp.

An old man creeps from out the woods,
   Breaking the vine's entangling spell;
He thrids the jungle's solitudes,
   O'er bamboos rotting where they fell;
Slow down the tiger's path he wends
Where at the pool the jungle ends.

No moss-greened alley tells the trace
   Of his lone step, no sound is stirred,
Even when his tawny hands displace
   The boughs, that backward sweep unheard

His way as noiseless as the trail
Of the swift snake and pilgrim snail.

The old snake-charmer,—once he played
   Soft music for the serpent's ear,
But now his cunning hand is stayed;
   He knows the hour of death is near.
And all that live in brake and bough,
All know the brand is on his brow.

Yet where his soul is he must go:
   He crawls along from tree to tree.
The old snake-charmer, doth he know
   If snake or beast of prey he be?
Bewildered at the pool he lies
And sees as through a serpent's eyes.

Weeds wove with white-flowered lily crops
   Drink of the pool, and serpents hie
To the thin brink as noonday drops,
   And in the froth-daubed rushes lie.
There rests he now with fastened breath
'Neath a kind sun to bask in death.

The pool is bright with glossy dyes
   And cast-up bubbles of decay:
A green death-leaven overlies
   Its mottled scum, where shadows play

As the snake's hollow coil, fresh shed,
Rolls in the wind across its bed.

No more the wily note is heard
   From his full flute—the riving air
That tames the snake, decoys the bird,
   Worries the she-wolf from her lair.
Fain would he bid its parting breath
Drown in his ears the voice of death.

Still doth his soul's vague longing skim
   The pool beloved: he hears the hiss
That siffles at the sedgy rim,
   Recalling days of former bliss,
And the death-drops, that fall in showers,
Seem honied dews from shady flowers.

There is a rustle of the breeze
   And twitter of the singing bird;
He snatches at the melodies
   And his faint lips again are stirred:
The olden sounds are in his ears;
But still the snake its crest uprears.

His eyes are swimming in the mist
   That films the earth like serpent's breath:
And now,—as if a serpent hissed,—
   The husky whisperings of Death

Fill ear and brain—he looks around—
Serpents seem matted o'er the ground.

Soon visions of past joys bewitch
   His crafty soul; his hands would set
Death's snare, while now his fingers twitch
   The tasselled reed as 'twere his net.
But his thin lips no longer fill
The woods with song; his flute is still.

Those lips still quaver to the flute,
   But fast the life-tide ebbs away;
Those lips now quaver and are mute,
   But nature throbs in breathless play:
Birds are in open song, the snakes
Are watching in the silent brakes.

In sudden fear of snares unseen
   The birds like crimson sunset swarm,
All gold and purple, red and green,
   And seek each other for the charm.
Lizards dart up the feathery trees
Like shadows of a rainbow breeze.

The wildered birds again have rushed
   Into the charm,—it is the hour
When the shrill forest-note is hushed,
   And they obey the serpent's power,—

Drawn to its gaze with troubled whirr,
As by the thread of falconer.

As 'twere to feed, on slanting wings
   They drop within the serpent's glare:
Eyes flashing fire in burning rings
   Which spread into the dazzled air;
They flutter in the glittering coils;
The charmer dreads the serpent's toils.

While Music swims away in death
   Man's spell is passing to his slaves:
The snake feeds on the charmer's breath,
   The vulture screams, the parrot raves,
The lone hyena laughs and howls,
The tiger from the jungle growls.

Then mounts the eagle—flame-flecked folds
   Belt its proud plumes; a feather falls:
He hears the death-cry, he beholds
   The king-bird in the serpent's thralls,
He looks with terror on the feud,—
And the sun shines through dripping blood.

The deadly spell a moment gone—
   Birds, from a distant Paradise,
Strike the winged signal and have flown,
   Trailing rich hues through azure skies:

The serpent falls; like demon wings
The far-out-branching cedar swings.

The wood swims round; the pool and skies
    Have met; the death-drops down that cheek
Fall faster; for the serpent's eyes
    Grow human, and the charmer's seek.
A gaze like man's directs the dart
Which now is buried at his heart.

The monarch of the world is cold:
    The charm he bore has passed away:
The serpent gathers up its fold
    To wind about its human prey.
The red mouth darts a dizzy sting,
And clenches the eternal ring.

AUBREY DE VERE
Born 1814

SONG

When I was young, I said to Sorrow,
  "Come, and I will play with thee" :—
    He is near me now all day;
    And at night returns to say,
"I will come again to-morrow,
  I will come and stay with thee."

Through the woods we walk together;
  His soft footsteps rustle nigh me;
    To shield an unregarded head,
    He hath built a winter shed;
And all night in rainy weather,
  I hear his gentle breathings by me.

From "ODE ON THE ASCENT OF THE ALPS"

All night as in my dreams I lay
  The shout of torrents without number
Was in my ears—"Away, away,
  No time have we for slumber!
The star-beams in our eddies play—
  The moon is set: away, away!"
And round the hills in tumult borne
  Through echoing caves and gorges rocking,
The voices of the night and morn
  Are crying louder in their scorn,
My tedious languor mocking.
  Alas! in vain man's wearied limbs would rise
To join in elemental ecstasies!

"But thou, O Muse, our heavenly mate,
Unclogged art thou by fleshly weight!
Ascend; upbearing my desire
Among the mountains higher and higher.
Leap from the glen upon the forest—
  Leap from the forest on the snow:
And while from snow to cloud thou soarest
  Look back on me below:
Where from the glacier bursts the river
  With iron clang, pursue it ever;

Where Eagles through the tempest break,
Float forward in their viewless wake;
Where sunbeams gild the icy spire
Fling from thy tresses fire on fire."

I spake—Behold her o'er the broad lake flying:
  Like a great Angel missioned to bestow
Some boon on men beneath in sadness lying:
  The waves are murmuring silver murmurs low:
    Beneath the curdling wind
Green through the shades the waters rush and roll,
(Or whitened only by the unfrequent shoal)
Till two dark hills, with darker yet behind,
Confront them,—purple mountains almost black,
  Each behind each self-folded and withdrawn
Beneath the umbrage of yon cloudy rack—
    That orange gleam! 'tis dawn!
Onward! the swan's flight with the eagle's blending,
On, wingèd Muse; still forward and ascending!

That mighty sweep, one orbit of her flight,
Has overcurved the mountain's barrier height:
She sinks, she speeds on prosperous wing prevailing,
(Broad lights below and changeful shadows sailing)
Over a vale upon whose breadth may shine
  Not noontide suns alone, but suns of even,
Warming the gray fields in their soft decline,
  The green streams flushing with the hues of heaven.

In vain those Shepherds call; they cannot wake
　　The echoes on this wide and cultured plain,
Where spreads the river now into a lake,
　　Now curves through walnut meads its golden chain,
　　　　In-isling here and there some spot
　　　　With orchard, hive, and one fair cot:
　　　　Or children dragging from their boat
Into the flood some reverend goat—
O happy valley! cradle soft and deep
　　　　For blissful life, calm sleep,
And leisure, and affections free and wide,
Give me yon plough, that I with thee may bide!
　　　　Or climb those stages, cot-bestrown,
　　　　Vast steps of Summer's mountain-throne,
Terrace o'er terrace rising, line o'er line,
Swathed in the light wreaths of the elaborate vine.
　　　　On yonder loftiest steep, the last
　　　　　　From whose green base the gray rocks rise,
　　　　In random circle idly cast
　　　　　　A happy household lies.
　　　　There rests the grandsire: round his feet
　　　　The children some old tale entreat,
　　　　And while he speaks supply each word
　　　　Forgotten, altered, or ill heard.
　　　　In yonder brake reclines a maid,
　　　　Her locks a lover's fingers braid—

Fair, fearless maiden! cause for fear
Is none, though he alone were near:
Indulge at will thy sweet security!
He doth but that bold front incline
And all those wind-tossed curls on thine
To catch from thy fresh lips their mountain purity!

LYCIUS

Lycius! the female race is all the same!
All variable, as the Poets tell us;
Mad through caprice—half way 'twixt men and
    children!

Acasta, mildest late of all our maids,
Colder and calmer than a sacred well,
Is now more changed than Spring has changed these
    woods;
Hers is the fault, not mine. Yourself shall judge

From Epidaurus, where for three long days
With Nicias I had stayed, honouring the God,
If strength might thus mine aged sire renerve,
Last evening we returned. The way was dull

And vexed with mountains: tired ere long was I
From warding off the oleander boughs
Which, as my comrade o'er the stream's dry bed
Pushed on, closed backward on my mule and me.
The flies maintained a melody unblest,
While Nicias, of his wreath Nemean proud,
Sang of the Satyrs and the Nymphs all day
Like one by Esculapius fever-smitten.
Arrived at eve, we bathed; and drank, and ate
Of figs and olives till our souls exulted:
Lastly we slept like Gods. While morning shone,
So filled was I with weariness and sleep
That as a log till noon I lay, then rose,
And in the bath-room sat. While there I languished
Reading that old, divine and holy tale
Of sad Ismenè and Antigonè,
Two warm, soft hands around me sudden flung
Closed both my eyes; and a clear, shrill, sweet laughter
Told me that she it was, Acasta's self,
That brake upon my dreams. "What would you, child?"
"Child, child!" Acasta cried, "I am no child—
You do me wrong in calling me a child!
Come with me to the willowy river's brim:
There read, if you must read."
       Her eyes not less

Than hands uplifted me, and forth we strayed.
O'er all the Argolic plain Apollo's shafts
So fiercely fell, methought the least had slain
A second Python.   From that theatre
Hewn in the rock the Argive tumult rolled :
Before the fane of Juno seven vast oxen
Lowed loud, denouncing Heaven ere yet they fell :
While from the hill-girt meadows rose a scent
So rich, the salt sea odours vainly strove
To pierce those fumes it curled about my brain,
And sting the nimbler spirits.   Nodding I watched
The pale herbs from the parchèd bank that trailed
Bathing delighted in voluptuous cold,
And scarcely swayed by that slow winding stream :
I heard a sigh—I asked not whence it came.
At last a breeze went by, to glossy waves
Rippling the steely flood : I noted then
The reflex of the poplar stem thereon
Curled into spiral wreaths, and toward me darting
Like a long, shining water-snake : I laughed
To see its restlessness.   Acasta cried,
" Read—if you will not speak—or look at me ! "
Unconsciously I glanced upon the page,
Bent o'er it, and begun to chaunt that song,
" Favoured by Love are they that love not deeply,"
When, leaping from my side, she snatched the book,
Into the river dashed it, bounded by,

And, no word spoken, left me there alone.

Lycius! I see you smile; but know you not
Nothing is trifling which the Muse records,
And lovers love to muse on? Let the Gods
Act as to them seems fitting. Hermes loved—
Phœbus loved also—but the hearts of Gods
Are everlasting like the sun and stars,
Their loves as transient as the clouds. For me
A peaceful life is all I seek, and far
Removed from cares and all the female kind!

THE CAMPO SANTO AT PISA

I

There needs not choral song, nor organs pealing:
This mighty cloister of itself inspires
Thoughts breathed like hymns from spiritual choirs;
While shades and lights, in soft succession stealing,
Along it creep, now veiling, now revealing
Strange forms, here traced by Painting's earliest sires,
Angels with palms; and purgatorial fires;
And Saints caught up, and demons round them reeling
Love, long remembering those she could not save,

Here hung the cradle of Italian Art:
Faith rocked it; hence, like hermit child, went forth
That heaven-born Power which beautified the earth:
She perished when the world had lured her heart
From her true friends, Religion and the grave.

II

Lament not thou: the cold winds, as they pass
Through the ribbed fret-work with low sigh or moan,
Lament enough; let them lament alone,
Counting the sere leaves of the innumerous grass
With thin, soft sound like one prolonged—"alas!"
Spread thou thy hands on sun-touched vase, or stone
That yet retains the warmth of sunshine gone,
And drink warm solace from the ponderous mass.
Gaze not around thee. Monumental marbles,
Time-clouded frescoes, mouldering year by year,
Dim cells in which all day the night-bird warbles,
These things are sorrowful elsewhere, not here:
A mightier Power than Art's hath here her shrine:
Stranger! thou tread'st the soil of Palestine!

PHILIP JAMES BAILEY

Born 1816

From "FESTUS"

Oh for the young heart like a fountain playing,
Flinging its bright fresh feelings up to the skies
It loves and strives to reach; strives, loves in vain.
It is of earth, and never meant for heaven;
Let us love both and die. The sphinx-like heart
Loathes life the moment that life's riddle is read.
The knot of our existence solved, all things
Loose-ended lie, and useless. Life is had,
And lo! we sigh, and say, can this be all?
It is not what we thought; it is very well,
But we want something more. There is but death.
And when we have said and seen, done, had, enjoyed
And suffered, maybe, all we have wished, or feared,
From fame to ruin, and from love to loathing,
There can come but one more change—try it—death.
Oh it is great to feel that nought of earth,
Hope, love, nor dread, nor care for what's to come,
Can check the royal lavishment of life;

But, like a streamer strown upon the wind,
We fling our souls to fate and to the future.
For to die young is youth's divinest gift;
To pass from one world fresh into another,
Ere change hath lost the charm of soft regret;
And feel the immortal impulse from within
Which makes the coming, life, cry alway, on!
And follow it while strong, is heaven's last mercy.
There is a fire-fly in the south, but shines
When on the wing. So is't with mind. When once
We rest, we darken. On! saith God to the soul,
As unto the earth for ever. On it goes,
A rejoicing native of the infinite,
As is a bird, of air; an orb, of heaven.

FREDERICK LOCKER-LAMPSON
Born 1821

THE UNREALIZED IDEAL

My only Love is always near,—
  In country or in town
I see her twinkling feet, I hear
  The whisper of her gown.

She foots it ever fair and young,
  Her locks are tied in haste,
And one is o'er her shoulder flung
  And hangs below her waist.

She ran before me in the meads;
  And down this world-worn track
She leads me on; but while she leads
  She never gazes back.

And yet her voice is in my dreams,
  To witch me more and more;
That wooing voice! Ah me, it seems
  Less near me than of yore.

Lightly I sped when hope was high,
  And youth beguiled the chase;
I follow—follow still; but I
  Shall never see her Face.

AT HER WINDOW

Ah, Minstrel, how strange is
  The carol you sing!
Let Psyche, who ranges
  The garden of Spring,
Remember the changes
  December will bring.

Beating Heart! we come again
  Where my Love reposes:
This is Mabel's window-pane;
  These are Mabel's roses.

Is she nested? Does she kneel
  In the twilight stilly,
Lily clad from throat to heel,
  She, my Virgin Lily?

Soon the wan, the wistful stars,
  Fading, will forsake her;
Elves of light, on beamy bars,
  Whisper then, and wake her.

Let this friendly pebble plead
    At her flowery grating;
If she hear me will she heed?
    Mabel, I am waiting.

Mabel will be deck'd anon,
    Zoned in bride's apparel;
Happy zone! Oh hark to yon
    Passion-shaken carol!

Sing thy song, thou trancèd Thrush,
    Pipe thy best, thy clearest;—
Hush, her lattice moves, O hush—
    Dearest Mabel!—dearest . . .

LOULOU AND HER CAT

You shake your saucy curls, and vow
I build no airy castles now;
You smile, and you are thinking too,—
He's nothing else on earth to do.

Good pastry is vended
    In Citè Fadette;
Maison Pons can make splendid
    Brioche and *galette.*

M'sieu Pons is so fat that
    He's laid on the shelf;
Madame had a Cat that
    Was fat as herself.

Long hair, soft as satin,
    A musical purr,
'Gainst the window she'd flatten
    Her delicate fur.

I drove Lou to see what
    Our neighbours were at,—
In rapture, cried she, " What
    An exquisite Cat !

" What whiskers ! She's purring
    All over. Regale
Our eyes, *Puss,* by stirring
    Your feathery tail !

" *M'sieu Pons,* will you sell her ? "
    " *Ma femme est sortie,*
Your offer I'll tell her ;
    But—will she ? " says he.

Yet *Pons* was persuaded
    To part with the prize :

(Our bargain was aided,
  My Lou, by your eyes!)

From his *légitime* save him,—
  My spouse I prefer,
For I warrant *his* gave him
  Un mauvais quart d'heure.

I am giving a pleasant
  Grimalkin to Lou,
—Ah, *Puss*, what a present
  I'm giving to you!

COVENTRY PATMORE

Born 1823

FROM "THE ANGEL IN THE HOUSE"

I

LOVE'S PERVERSITY

How strange a thing a lover seems
    To animals that do not love!
Lo, where he walks and talks in dreams,
    And flouts us with his Lady's glove;
How foreign is the garb he wears;
    And how his great devotion mocks
Our poor propriety, and scares
    The undevout with paradox!
His soul, through scorn of worldly care,
    And great extremes of sweet and gall,
And musing much on all that's fair,
    Grows witty and fantastical;
He sobs his joy and sings his grief,
    And evermore finds such delight
In simply picturing his relief,
    That 'plaining seems to cure his plight;

He makes his sorrow, when there's none;
　His fancy blows both cold and hot;
Next to the wish that she'll be won,
　His first hope is that she may not;
He sues, yet deprecates consent;
　Would she be captured she must fly;
She looks too happy and content,
　For whose least pleasure he would die;
Oh, cruelty, she cannot care
　For one to whom she's always kind!
He says he's nought, but, oh, despair,
　If he's not Jove to her fond mind!
He's jealous if she pets a dove,
　She must be his with all her soul;
Yet 'tis a postulate in love
　That part is greater than the whole;
And all his apprehension's stress,
　When he's with her, regards her hair,
Her hand, a ribbon of her dress,
　As if his life were only there;
Because she's constant, he will change
　And kindest glances coldly meet,
And, all the time he seems so strange,
　His soul is fawning at her feet;
Of smiles and simple heaven grown tired,
　He wickedly provokes her tears,
And when she weeps, as he desired,

Falls slain with ecstacies of fears ;
He blames her, though she has no fault,
   Except the folly to be his ;
He worships her, the more to exalt
   The profanation of a kiss ;
Health's his disease ; he's never well
   But when his paleness shames her rose ;
His faith's a rock-built citadel,
   Its sign a flag that each way blows ;
His o'erfed fancy frets and fumes ;
   And Love, in him, is fierce, like Hate,
And ruffles his ambrosial plumes
   Against the bars of time and fate.

II

THE REVELATION

An idle poet, here and there,
   Looks round him ; but, for all the rest,
The world, unfathomably fair,
   Is duller than a witling's jest.
Love wakes men, once a lifetime each ;
   They lift their heavy lids, and look ;
And, lo, what one sweet page can teach,
   They read with joy, then shut the book.

And some give thanks, and some blaspheme,
    And most forget; but, either way,
That and the Child's unheeded dream
    Is all the light of all their day.

THE TOYS

My little Son, who look'd from thoughtful eyes,
And moved and spoke in quiet grown-up wise,
Having my law the seventh time disobey'd,
I struck him, and dismiss'd
With hard words and unkiss'd,
(His Mother, who was patient, being dead.)
Then, fearing lest his grief should hinder sleep,
I visited his bed,
But found him slumbering deep,
With darken'd eyelids, and their lashes yet
From his late sobbing wet.
And I, with moan,
Kissing away his tears, left others of my own;
For, on a table drawn beside his head,
He had put, within his reach,
A box of counters and a red-veined stone,
A piece of glass abraded by the beach

And six or seven shells,
A bottle with bluebells
And two French copper coins, ranged there with
    careful art,
To comfort his sad heart.
So when that night I pray'd
To God, I wept, and said:
Ah, when at last we lie with tranced breath,
Not vexing Thee in death,
And Thou rememberest of what toys
We made our joys,
How weakly understood,
Thy great commanded good,
Then, fatherly not less
Than I whom Thou hast moulded from the clay,
Thou'lt leave Thy wrath, and say,
" I will be sorry for their childishness."

DEPARTURE

It was not like your great and gracious ways!
Do you, that have nought other to lament,
Never, my Love, repent
Of how, that July afternoon,

You went,
With sudden, unintelligible phrase,
And frighten'd eye,
Upon your journey of so many days,
Without a single kiss, or a good-bye?
I knew, indeed, that you were parting soon;
And so we sate, within the low sun's rays,
You whispering to me, for your voice was weak,
Your harrowing praise.
Well, it was well,
To hear you such things speak,
And I could tell
What made your eyes a growing gloom of love,
As a warm South-wind sombres a March grove.
And it was like your great and gracious ways
To turn your talk on daily things, my Dear,
Lifting the luminous, pathetic lash
To let the laughter flash,
Whilst I drew near,
Because you spoke so low that I could scarcely hear.
But all at once to leave me at the last,
More at the wonder than the loss aghast,
With huddled, unintelligible phrase,
And frightened eye,
And go your journey of all days
With not one kiss, or a good-bye,

And the only loveless look the look with which you
    pass'd;
'Twas all unlike your great and gracious ways.

THE AZALEA

There, where the sun shines first
Against our room,
She train'd the gold Azalea, whose perfume
She, Spring-like, from her breathing grace dispersed.
Last night the delicate crests of saffron bloom,
For that their dainty likeness watch'd and nurst,
Were just at point to burst.
At dawn I dream'd, O God, that she was dead,
And groan'd aloud upon my wretched bed,
And waked, ah, God, and did not waken her,
But lay, with eyes still closed,
Perfectly bless'd in the delicious sphere
By which I knew so well that she was near,
My heart to speechless thankfulness composed.
Till 'gan to stir
A dizzy somewhat in my troubled head—
It *was* the azalea's breath, and she *was* dead!
The warm night had the lingering buds disclosed,

And I had fall'n asleep with to my breast
A chance-found letter press'd
In which she said,
" So, till to-morrow eve, my Own, adieu!
Parting's well-paid with soon again to meet,
Soon in your arms to feel so small and sweet,
Sweet to myself that am so sweet to you!"

WILLIAM ALEXANDER

Born 1824

A VISION OF OXFORD

Methought I met a Lady yestereven ;
  A passionless grief, that had nor tear nor wail,
Sat on her pure proud face, that gleam'd to Heaven,
  White as a moon-lit sail.

She spake : "On this pale brow are looks of youth,
  Yet angels listening on the argent floor
Know that these lips have been proclaiming truth,
  Nine hundred years and more :

And Isis knows what time-grey towers rear'd up,
  Gardens and groves and cloister'd halls are mine,
Where quaff my sons from many a myrrhine cup
  Draughts of ambrosial wine.

He knows how night by night my lamps are lit,
  How day by day my bells are ringing clear,

Mother of ancient lore, and Attic wit,
    And discipline severe.

"It may be long ago my dizzied brain
    Enchanted swam beneath Rome's master spell,
Till like light tinctured by the painted pane
    Thought in *her* colours fell.

"Yet when the great old tongue with strong effect
    Woke from the sepulchre across the sea,
The subtler spell of Grecian intellect
    Work'd mightily in me.

"Time pass'd—my groves were full of warlike stirs;
    The student's heart was with the merry spears,
Or keeping measure to the clanking spurs
    Of Rupert's Cavaliers.

'All those long ages, like a holy mother
    I rear'd my children to a lore sublime,
Picking up fairer shells than any other
    Along the shores of Time.

"And must I speak at last of sensual sleep,
    The dull forgetfulness of aimless years?
O! let me turn away my head and weep
    Than Rachel's bitterer tears.

" Tears for the passionate hearts I might have won,
   Tears for the age with which I might have striven,
Tears for a hundred years of work undone,
      Crying like blood to Heaven.

" I have repented, and my glorious name
   Stands scutcheon'd round with blazonry more bright.
The wither'd rod, the emblem of my shame,
   Bloom'd blossoms in a night.

" And I have led my children on steep mountains
   By fine attraction of my spirit brought
Up to the dark inexplicable fountains
   That are the springs of thought:

" Led them—where on the old poetic shore
   The flowers that change not with the changing moon
Breathe round young hearts, as breathes the sycamore
   About the bees in June.

" And I will bear them as on eagle's wings,
   To leave them bow'd before the sapphire Throne,
High o'er the haunts where dying pleasure sings
   With sweet and swanlike tone.

"And I will lead the age's great expansions,
  Progressive circles toward thought's Sabbath
        rest,
And point beyond them to the 'many mansions'
  Where Christ is with the blest.

"Am I not pledged, who gave my bridal ring
  To that old man, heroic, strong, and true,
Whose grey-hair'd virtue was a nobler thing
      Than even Waterloo?

"Surely that spousal morn my chosen ones
  Felt their hearts moving to mysterious calls,
And the old pictures of my sainted sons
      Look'd brighter from the walls.

"He sleeps at last—no wind's tempestuous breath
  Play'd a Dead March upon the moaning billow,
What time God's Angel visited with death
      The old Field-Marshal's pillow.

"There was no omen of a great disaster
  Where castled Walmer stands beside the shore;
The evening clouds, like pillar'd alabaster,
      Hung huge and silent o'er.

" The moon in brightness walk'd the 'fleecy rack,'
  Walk'd up and down among the starry fires,
Heaven's great cathedral was not hung with black
  Up to its topmost spires !

" But mine own Isis kept a solemn chiming,
  A silver Requiescat all night long,
And mine old trees, with all their leaves, were timing
  The sorrow of the song.

" And through mine angel-haunted aisles of beauty
  From grand old organs gush'd a music dim,
Lauds for a champion who had done his duty.
  I knew they were for *him* !"

CHRISTINA GEORGINA ROSSETTI

Born 1830

AMOR MUNDI

"O where are you going with your love-locks flowing,
   On the west wind blowing along this valley track?"
"The down-hill path is easy, come with me an it
     please ye,
   We shall escape the up-hill by never turning back."

So they two went together in glowing August weather,
   The honey-breathing heather lay to their left and
     right;
And dear she was to doat on, her swift feet seemed to
     float on
   The air like soft twin pigeons too sportive to alight.

"Oh, what is that in heaven where grey cloud-flakes
     are seven,
   Where blackest clouds hang riven just at the rainy
     skirt?"

"Oh, that's a meteor sent us, a message dumb, portentous,
An undeciphered solemn signal of help or hurt."

"Oh, what is that glides quickly where velvet flowers grow thickly,
Their scent comes rich and sickly?" "A scaled and hooded worm."
"Oh, what's that in the hollow, so pale I quake to follow?"
"Oh, that's a thin dead body which waits the eternal term."

"Turn again, O my sweetest,—turn again, false and fleetest:
This beaten way thou beatest, I fear is hell's own track."
"Nay, too steep for hill mounting; nay, too late for cost counting:
This down-hill path is easy, but there's no turning back."

UP-HILL

Does the road wind up-hill all the way?
   Yes, to the very end.
Will the day's journey take the whole long day?
   From morn to night, my friend.

But is there for the night a resting-place?
   A roof for when the slow dark hours begin.
May not the darkness hide it from my face?
   You cannot miss that inn.

Shall I meet other wayfarers at night?
   Those who have gone before.
Then must I knock, or call when just in sight?
   They will not keep you standing at the door.

Shall I find comfort, travel-sore and weak?
   Of labour you shall find the sum.
Will there be beds for me and all who seek?
   Yea, beds for all who come.

SONG

When I am dead, my dearest,
  Sing no sad songs for me;
Plant thou no roses at my head,
  No shady cypress tree:
Be the green grass above me
  With showers and dewdrops wet;
And if thou wilt, remember,
  And if thou wilt, forget.

I shall not see the shadows,
  I shall not feel the rain;
I shall not hear the nightingale
  Sing on, as if in pain:
And dreaming through the twilight
  That doth not rise nor set,
Haply I may remember,
  And haply may forget.

BIRD RAPTURES

The sunrise wakes the lark to sing,
   The moonrise wakes the nightingale.
Come darkness, moonrise, everything
   That is so silent, sweet, and pale,
   Come, so ye wake the nightingale.

Make haste to mount, thou wistful moon,
   Make haste to wake the nightingale:
Let silence set the world in tune
   To hearken to that wordless tale
   Which warbles from the nightingale.

O herald skylark, stay thy flight
   One moment, for a nightingale
Floods us with sorrow and delight.
   To-morrow thou shalt hoist the sail;
   Leave us to-night the nightingale.

NOBLE SISTERS

"Now did you mark a falcon,
   Sister dear, sister dear,
Flying toward my window
   In the morning cool and clear?

With jingling bells about her neck,
   But what beneath her wing?
It may have been a ribbon,
   Or it may have been a ring."—
      "I marked a falcon swooping
         At the break of day:
      And for your love, my sister-dove,
         I 'frayed the thief away."—

"Or did you spy a ruddy hound,
   Sister fair and tall,
Went snuffing round my garden bound,
   Or crouched by my bower wall?
With a silken leash about his neck;
   But in his mouth may be
A chain of gold and silver links,
   Or a letter writ to me."—
      "I heard a hound, high-born sister,
         Stood baying at the moon:
      I rose and drove him from your wall
         Lest you should wake too soon."—

"Or did you meet a pretty page
   Sat swinging on the gate;
Sat whistling whistling like a bird,
   Or may be slept too late:
With eaglets broidered on his cap,
   And eaglets on his glove?

If you had turned his pockets out,
　　You had found some pledge of love."—
　　　"I met him at this daybreak,
　　　　Scarce the east was red :
　　　Lest the creaking gate should anger you,
　　　　I packed him home to bed."—

"Oh patience, sister. Did you see
　　A young man tall and strong,
Swift-footed to uphold the right
　　And to uproot the wrong,
Come home across the desolate sea
　　To woo me for his wife?
And in his heart my heart is locked,
　　And in his life my life."—
　　　"I met a nameless man, sister,
　　　　Who loitered round our door :
　　　I said : Her husband loves her much.
　　　　And yet she loves him more."—

"Fie, sister, fie! a wicked lie,
　　A lie, a wicked lie,
I have none other love but him,
　　Nor will have till I die.
And you have turned him from our door,
　　And stabbed him with a lie :
I will go seek him thro' the world
　　In sorrow till I die."—

"Go seek in sorrow, sister,
　　And find in sorrow too:
If thus you shame our father's name
　　My curse go forth with you."

AT HOME

When I was dead, my spirit turned
　　To seek the much-frequented house:
I passed the door, and saw my friends
　　Feasting beneath green orange-boughs;
From hand to hand they pushed the wine,
　　They sucked the pulp of plum and peach;
They sang, they jested, and they laughed,
　　For each was loved of each.

I listened to their honest chat:
　　Said one: "To-morrow we shall be
Plod plod along the featureless sands,
　　And coasting miles and miles of sea."
Said one: "Before the turn of tide
　　We will achieve the eyrie-seat."
Said one: "To-morrow shall be like
　　To-day, but much more sweet."

"To-morrow," said they, strong with hope,
  And dwelt upon the pleasant way:
"To-morrow," cried they one and all,
  While no one spoke of yesterday.
Their life stood full at blessed noon;
  I, only I, had passed away:
"To-morrow and to-day," they cried:
  I was of yesterday.

I shivered comfortless, but cast
  No chill across the tablecloth;
I all-forgotten shivered, sad
  To stay and yet to part how loth:
I passed from the familiar room,
  I who from love had passed away,
Like the remembrance of a guest
  That tarrieth but a day.

DREAM LAND

Where sunless rivers weep
Their waves into the deep,
She sleeps a charmèd sleep:
  Awake her not.

Led by a single star,
She came from very far
To seek where shadows are
    Her pleasant lot.

She left the rosy morn,
She left the fields of corn,
For twilight cold and lorn
    And water springs.
Through sleep, as through a veil,
She sees the sky look pale,
And hears the nightingale
    That sadly sings.

Rest, rest, a perfect rest
Shed over brow and breast;
Her face is toward the west,
    The purple land.
She cannot see the grain
Ripening on hill and plain;
She cannot feel the rain
    Upon her hand.

Rest, rest, for evermore
Upon a mossy shore;
Rest, rest at the heart's core
    Till time shall cease:

Sleep that no pain shall wake;
Night that no morn shall break
Till joy shall overtake
    Her perfect peace.

AFTER DEATH

SONNET

The curtains were half drawn, the floor was swept
  And strewn with rushes, rosemary and may
  Lay thick upon the bed on which I lay,
Where through the lattice ivy-shadows crept.
He leaned above me, thinking that I slept
  And could not hear him; but I heard him say:
  "Poor child, poor child:" and as he turned away
Came a deep silence, and I knew he wept.
He did not touch the shroud, or raise the fold
  That hid my face, or take my hand in his,
    Or ruffle the smooth pillows for my head:
  He did not love me living; but once dead
  He pitied me; and very sweet it is
To know he still is warm though I am cold.

From "TIME FLIES"

I

My love whose heart is tender said to me,
   "A moon lacks light except her sun befriend her.
Let us keep tryst in heaven, dear Friend," said she,
   My love whose heart is tender.

   From such a loftiness no words could bend her;
Yet still she spoke of "us," and spoke as "we,"
   Her hope substantial while my hope grew slender.

Now keeps she tryst beyond earth's utmost sea,
   Wholly at rest tho' storms should toss and rend her,
And still she keeps my heart and keeps its key,
   My love whose heart is tender.

II

   Where shall I find a white rose blowing?—
     Out in the garden where all sweets be.—
   But out in my garden the snow was snowing
     And never a white rose opened for me.

Nought but snow and a wind were blowing
And snowing.

Where shall I find a blush rose blushing?—
　　On the garden wall or the garden bed.—
But out in my garden the rain was rushing
　　And never a blush rose raised its head.
Nothing glowing, flushing or blushing;
Rain rushing.

Where shall I find a red rose budding?—
　　Out in the garden where all things grow.—
But out in my garden a flood was flooding
　　And never a red rose began to blow.
Out in a flooding what should be budding?
All flooding!

Now is winter and now is sorrow,
　　No roses but only thorns to-day:
Thorns will put on roses to-morrow,
　　Winter and sorrow scudding away.
No more winter and no more sorrow
To-morrow.

III

If love is not worth loving, then life is not worth living,
  Nor aught is worth remembering but well forgot,
For store is not worth storing and gifts are not worth
    giving,
  If love is not ;

  And idly cold is death-cold, and life-heat idly hot,
And vain is any offering and vainer our receiving,
  And vanity of vanities is all our lot.

Better than life's heaving heart is death's heart un-
    heaving,
  Better than the opening leaves are the leaves that rot,
For there is nothing left worth achieving or retrieving,
  If love is not.

IV

Of all the downfalls in the world,
  The flutter of an Autumn leaf
  Grows grievous by suggesting grief:

Who thought, when Spring was first unfurled,
Of this? The wide world lay empearled;
Who thought of frost that nips the world?
     Sigh on, my ditty.

There lurk a hundred subtle stings
 To prick us in our daily walk:
 An apple cankered on its stalk,
A robin snared for all his wings,
A voice that sang but never sings;
Yea, sight or sound or silence stings.
     Kind Lord, show mercy.

SIR EDWIN ARNOLD

Born 1832

From "THE LIGHT OF ASIA"

But on another day the King said, "Come,
Sweet son! and see the pleasaunce of the spring,
And how the fruitful earth is wooed to yield
Its riches to the reaper; how my realm—
Which shall be thine when the pile flames for me—
Feeds all its mouths and keeps the King's chest filled.
Fair is the season with new leaves, bright blooms,
Green grass, and cries of plough-time." So they rode
Into a land of wells and gardens, where,
All up and down the rich red loam, the steers
Strained their strong shoulders in the creaking yoke
Dragging the ploughs; the fat soil rose and rolled
In smooth long waves back from the plough; who drove
Planted both feet upon the leaping share
To make the furrow deep; among the palms
The tinkle of the rippling water rang,
And where it ran the glad earth 'broidered it

With balsams and the spears of lemon-grass.
Elsewhere were sowers who went forth to sow;
And all the jungle laughed with nesting-songs,
And all the thickets rustled with small life
Of lizard, bee, beetle, and creeping things
Pleased at the spring-time. In the mango-sprays
The sun-birds flashed; alone at his green forge
Toiled the loud coppersmith; bee-eaters hawked,
Chasing the purple butterflies; beneath,
Striped squirrels raced, the mynas perked and picked,
The seven brown sisters chattered in the thorn,
The pied fish-tiger hung above the pool,
The egrets stalked among the buffaloes,
The kites sailed circles in the golden air;
About the painted temple peacocks flew,
The blue doves cooed from every well, far off
The village drums beat for some marriage-feast;
All things spoke peace and plenty, and the Prince
Saw and rejoiced. But, looking deep, he saw
The thorns which grew upon this rose of life:
How the swart peasant sweated for his wage,
Toiling for leave to live; and how he urged
The great-eyed oxen through the flaming hours,
Goading their velvet flanks: then marked he, too,
How lizard fed on ant, and snake on him,
And kite on both; and how the fish-hawk robbed
The fish-tiger of that which it had seized;

The shrike chasing the bulbul, which did hunt
The jewelled butterflies; till everywhere
Each slew a slayer and in turn was slain,
Life living upon death. So the fair show
Veiled one vast, savage, grim conspiracy
Of mutual murder, from the worm to man,
Who himself kills his fellow; seeing which—
The hungry ploughman and his labouring kine,
Their dewlaps blistered with the bitter yoke,
The rage to live which makes all living strife—
The Prince Siddârtha sighed. " Is this," he said,
" That happy earth they brought me forth to see?
How salt with sweat the peasant's bread! how hard
The oxen's service! in the brake how fierce
The war of weak and strong! i' th' air what plots!
No refuge e'en in water. Go aside
A space, and let me muse on what ye show."

TO A PAIR OF EGYPTIAN SLIPPERS

Tiny slippers of gold and green,
   Tied with a mouldering golden cord!
What pretty feet they must have been
   When Cæsar Augustus was Egypt's lord!

Somebody graceful and fair you were!
  Not many girls could dance in these!
When did your shoemaker make you, dear,
  Such a nice pair of Egyptian "threes"?

Where were you measured? In Saïs, or On,
  Memphis, or Thebes, or Pelusium?
Fitting them neatly your brown toes upon,
  Lacing them deftly with finger and thumb,
I seem to see you!—so long ago,
  Twenty-one centuries, less or more!
And here are your sandals : yet none of us know
  What name, or fortune, or face you bore.

Your lips would have laughed, with a rosy scorn,
  If the merchant, or slave-girl, had mockingly said,
" The feet will pass, but the shoes they have worn
  Two thousand years onward Time's road shall tread,
And still be footgear as good as new!"
  To think that calf-skin, gilded and stitched,
Should Rome and the Pharaohs outlive—and you
  Be gone, like a dream, from the world you bewitched!

Not that we mourn you! 'Twere too absurd!
  You have been such a very long while away!
Your dry spiced dust would not value one word
  Of the soft regrets that my verse could say.

Sorrow and Pleasure, and Love and Hate,
  If you ever felt them, have vaporised hence
To this odour—so subtle and delicate—
  Of myrrh, and cassia, and frankincense.

Of course they embalmed you! Yet not so sweet
  Were aloes and nard, as the youthful glow
Which Amenti stole when the small dark feet
  Wearied of treading our world below.
Look! it was flood-time in valley of Nile,
  Or a very wet day in the Delta, dear!
When your slippers tripped lightly their latest mile—
  The mud on the soles renders that fact clear.

You knew Cleopatra, no doubt! You saw
  Antony's galleys from Actium come.
But there! if questions could answers draw
  From lips so many a long age dumb,
I would not teaze you with history,
  Nor vex your heart for the men that were;
The one point to learn that would fascinate me
  Is, where and what are you to-day, my dear!

You died, believing in Horus and Pasht,
  Isis, Osiris, and priestly lore;
And found, of course, such theories smashed
  By actual fact on the heavenly shore.

What next did you do? Did you transmigrate?
   Have we seen you since, all modern and fresh?
Your charming soul—so I calculate—
   Mislaid its mummy, and sought new flesh.

Were you she whom I met at dinner last week,
   With eyes and hair of the Ptolemy black,
Who still of this find in the Fayoum would speak,
   And to Pharaohs and scarabs still carry us back?
A scent of lotus about her hung,
   And she had such a far-away wistful air
As of somebody born when the Earth was young;
   And she wore of gilt slippers a lovely pair.

Perchance you were married? These might have been
   Part of your *trousseau*—the wedding shoes;
And you laid them aside with the garments green,
   And painted clay Gods which a bride would use;
And, may be, to-day, by Nile's bright waters
   Damsels of Egypt in gowns of blue—
Great-great-great—very-great—grand-daughters
   Owe their shapely insteps to you!

But vainly I beat at the bars of the Past,
   Little green slippers with golden strings!
For all you can tell is that leather will last
   When loves, and delightings, and beautiful things

Have vanished, forgotten—No! not quite that!
I catch some gleam of the grace you wore
When you finished with Life's daily pit-a-pat,
   And left your shoes at Death's bedroom door.

You were born in the Egypt which did not doubt;
   You were never sad with our new-fashioned sorrows:
You were sure, when your play-days on Earth ran out,
   Of play-times to come, as we of our morrows!
Oh, wise little Maid of the Delta! I lay
   Your shoes in your mummy-chest back again,
And wish that one game we might merrily play
   At " Hunt the Slipper "—to see it all plain.

LEWIS MORRIS

Born 1833

AT LAST

Let me at last be laid
On that hillside I know which scans the vale,
Beneath the thick yews' shade,
For shelter when the rains and winds prevail.
It cannot be the eye
Is blinded when we die,
So that we know no more at all
The dawns increase, the evenings fall;
Shut up within a mouldering chest of wood
Asleep, and careless of our children's good.

Shall I not feel the spring,
The yearly resurrection of the earth,
Stir thro' each sleeping thing
With the fair throbbings and alarms of birth,
Calling at its own hour
On folded leaf and flower,
Calling the lamb, the lark, the bee,
Calling the crocus and anemone,

Calling new lustre to the maiden's eye,
And to the youth love and ambition high?

Shall I no more admire
The winding river kiss the daisied plain?
Nor see the dawn's cold fire
Steal downward from the rosy hills again?
Nor watch the frowning cloud,
Sublime with mutterings loud,
Burst on the vale, nor eves of gold,
Nor crescent moons, nor starlights cold,
Nor the red casements glimmer on the hill
At Yule-tides, when the frozen leas are still?

Or should my children's tread
Through Sabbath twilights, when the hymns are done,
Come softly overhead,
Shall no sweet quickening through my bosom run,
Till all my soul exhale
Into the primrose pale,
And every flower which springs above
Breathes a new perfume from my love;
And I shall throb, and stir, and thrill beneath
With a pure passion stronger far than death?

Sweet thought! fair, gracious dream,
Too fair and fleeting for our clearer view!

How should our reason deem
That those dear souls, who sleep beneath the blue
In rayless caverns dim,
'Mid ocean monsters grim,
Or whitening on the trackless sand,
Or with strange corpses on each hand
In battle-trench or city graveyard lie,
Break not their prison-bonds till time shall die?

Nay, 'tis not so indeed.
With the last fluttering of the failing breath
The clay-cold form doth breed
A viewless essence, far too fine for death;
And ere one voice can mourn,
On upward pinions borne,
They are hidden, they are hidden, in some thin air,
Far from corruption, far from care,
Where through a veil they view their former scene,
Only a little touched by what has been.

Touched but a little; and yet,
Conscious of every change that doth befal,
By constant change beset,
The creatures of this tiny whirling ball,
Filled with a higher being,
Dowered with a clearer seeing,
Risen to a vaster scheme of life,

To wider joys and nobler strife,
Viewing our little human hopes and fears
As we our children's fleeting smiles and tears.

Then, whether with fire they burn
This dwelling-house of mine when I am fled,
And in a marble urn
My ashes rest by my belovèd dead,
Or in the sweet cold earth
I pass from death to birth,
And pay kind Nature's life-long debt
In heart's-ease and in violet—
In charnel-yard or hidden ocean wave,
Where'er I lie, I shall not scorn my grave.

THE HOME ALTAR

Why should we seek at all to gain
By vigils, and in pain,
By lonely life and empty heart,
To set a soul apart
Within a cloistered cell,
For whom the precious, homely hearth would serve as
    well?

There, with the early breaking morn,
Ere quite the day is born,
The lustral waters flow serene,
And each again grows clean;
From sleep, as from a tomb,
Born to another dawn of joy, and hope, and doom.

There through the sweet and toilsome day,
To labour is to pray;
There love with kindly beaming eyes
Prepares the sacrifice;
And voice and innocent smile
Of childhood do our cheerful liturgies beguile.

There, at his chaste and frugal feast,
Love sitteth as a Priest;
And with mild eyes and mien sedate,
His deacons stand and wait;
And round the holy table
Paten and chalice range in order serviceable.

And when ere night, the vespers said,
Low lies each weary head,
What giveth He who gives them sleep,
But a brief death less deep?
Or what the fair dreams given
But ours who, daily dying, dream a happier heaven?

Then not within a cloistered wall
Will we expend our days ;
But dawns that break and eves that fall
Shall bring their dues of praise.
This best befits a Ruler always near,
This duteous worship mild, and reasonable fear.

From "GWEN"

EPILOGUE

The silent Forces of the World,
Time, Change, and Fate, deride us still ;
Nor ever from the hidden summit, furled,
Where sits the Eternal Will,
The clouds of Pain and Error rise
Before our straining eyes.

It is to-day as 'twas before,
From the far days when Man began to speak,
Ere Moses preached or Homer sung,
Ere Buddha's musing thought or Plato's silvery tongue.
We pace our destined path with failing footsteps weak ;
A little more we see, a little more

Of that great orb which shineth day and night
Through the high heaven, now hidden, now too bright,
The Sun to which the earth on which we are,
Life's labouring world, is as the feeblest star.

Nor this firm globe we know
Which lies beneath our feet;
Nor by what grades we have grown and yet shall grow,
Through chains of miracle, more and more complete;
By what decrees the watery earth
Compacted grew the womb of countless birth;
Nor, when the failing breath
Is taken by the frozen lips of Death,
Whither the Spoiler, fleeing with his prey,
The fluttering, wandering Wonder bears away.

The powers of Pain and Wrong,
Immeasurably strong,
Assail our souls, and chill with common doubt
Clear brain and heart devout:
War, Pestilence, and Famine, as of old,
The lust of the flesh, the baser lust of gold,
Vex us and harm us still;
Fire comes, and crash and wreck, and lives are shed
As if the Eternal Will itself were dead;

And sometimes Wrong and Right, the thing we fear,
The thing we cherish, draw confusedly near ;
We know not which to choose, we cannot separate
Our longing and our hate.

But Love the Conqueror, Love, Immortal Love,
Through the high heaven doth move,
Spurning the brute earth with his purple wings,
And from the great Sun brings
Some radiant beam to light the House of Life,
Sweetens our grosser thought, and makes us pure ;
And to a Higher Being doth mature
Our lower lives, and calms the ignoble strife,
And raises the dead life with his sweet breath,
And from the arms of Death
Soars with it to the eternal shore,
Where sight or thought of evil comes no more.

Love sitteth now above,
Enthroned in glory,
And yet hath deigned to move
Through life's sad story.
Fair Name, we are only thine !
Thou only art divine !
Be with us to the end, for there is none
But thou to bind together God and Man in one.

THE BEGINNINGS OF FAITH

All travail of high thought,
All secrets vainly sought,
All struggles for right, heroic, perpetually fought.

Faint gleams of purer fire,
Conquests of gross desire,
Whereby the fettered soul ascends continually higher.

Sweet cares for love or friend
Which ever heavenward tend,
Too deep and true and tender to have on earth their end.

Vile hearts malign and fell,
Lives which no tongue may tell,
So dark and dread and shameful that they breathe a present hell.

White mountain, deep-set lake,
Sea wastes which surge and break,
Fierce storms which, roaring from the north, the midnight forests shake.

Fair morns of summer days,
Rich harvest eves that raise
The soul and heart o'erburdened to an ecstasy of praise.

Low whispers, vague and strange,
Which through our being range,
Breathing perpetual presage of some mighty coming change.

These in the soul do breed
Thoughts which, at last, shall lead
To some clear, firm assurance of a satisfying creed.

THE ODE OF DECLINE

With forces well-nigh spent,
Uneasy or in pain,
Or brought to childish weakness once again,
With bodies shrunk and bent,
We come, if Fate so will, to cold decrepit age.
The book of Life lies open at its latest page.

Only four score of summers, and four score
Of winters, nothing more,

And then 'tis done.
We have spent our fruitful days beneath the sun ;
We come to a cold season and a bare,
Where little is sweet or fair.
We, who a few brief years ago,
Would passionately go
Across the fields of Life to meet the morn,
We are content, content, and not forlorn,
To lie upon our beds, and watch the Day
Which kissed the Eastern peaks, grow gradually grey.

Great Heaven, that Thou hast made our lives so brief
And swiftly spent!
We toil our little day and are content,
Though Time, the thief,
Stands at our side, and smiles his mystic smile.
We joy a little, we grieve a little while ;
We gain some little glimpse of Thy great laws,
Rolling in thunder through the voids of space ;
We gain to look a moment on Thy face,
Eternal Source and Cause!
And then, the night descending as a cloud,
We walk with aspect bowed,
And turn to earth and see our Life grow dark.
Was it for this the fiery spark
Of Thy Eternal Self, sown on the vast
And infinite abysses of the Past,

Revealed itself and made Creation rise
Before Thy Eternal Mind :
This little span of life, with purblind eyes
That grow completely blind ;
This little force of brain,
Holding dim thoughts sublime,
Too weak to withstand the treacheries of Time ;
This body bent and bowed in twain,
Soon racked by growing pain,
Which briefer far than is the life of the tree,
Springs as a flower and fades, and then must rot
And perish and be not,
Passing from mystery to mystery ?

It is a pain
To move through the old fields,—even though they lie
Before our eyes, we know that never again,
Where once our daily feet were used to pass
Amid the crested grass,
We any more shall wander till we die ;
Nor to the old grey church, with the tall spire,
Whose vane the sunsets fire,
Where once a little child, by kind hands led,
Would spell the scant memorials of the dead,—
Never again, or once alone,
When pain and Time are done.

The soaring thoughts of youth
Are dead and cold, the victories of Thought
Are no more prized or sought
By eyes which draw too near the face of Truth.
Whatever fruit or gain
Fate held in store,
To tempt the growing soul or brain,
Allures no more.
It is as the late Autumn, when the fields
Are bare of flower or fruit;
Nor charm nor profit the swept surface yields,
Sullen and mute;
So that a doubting mind might come to hold
The very soul and life were dead and cold.

But who can peer
Into another soul, or tell at all
What hidden energies befall
The aged lingering here?
When all the weary brain
Seems dull, the immeasurable fields of life
Lie open to the memory, and again
They know the youthful joys, the hurry and the strife,
And feel, but gentlier now, the ancient pain.
In the uneasy vigils of the night,
Before the tardy light;
Or, lonely days, when no young lives are by,

There come such long processions of the dead,
The buried lives and hopes of far-off years,
Spent joys and dried-up tears,
That round them stands a blessed company,
Holding high converse, though no word be said,
Till only what is past and gone doth seem
To live, and all the Present is a dream.

So may the wintry earth,
Holding her precious seeds within the ground,
Pause for the coming birth,
When like a clarion-note the Spring shall sound;
So may the roots which, buried deep
And safe within her sleep,
Whisper as 'twere, within, tales of the sun,—
Whisper of leaf and flower, of bee and bird,—
Till by a sudden glory stirred,
A mystic influence bids them rise,
Bursting the narrow sheath
And cerement of death,
And bloom as lilies again beneath the recovered skies.

ON A THRUSH SINGING IN AUTUMN

Sweet singer of the Spring, when the new world
Was filled with song and bloom, and the fresh year
Tripped, like a lamb playful and void of fear,
Through daisied grass and young leaves scarce unfurled,
Where is thy liquid voice
That all day would rejoice?
Where now thy clear and homely call,
Which from gray dawn to evening's chilling fall
Would echo from thin copse and tasselled brake,
For homely duty tuned and love's dear sake?

The spring-tide passed, high summer soon should come.
The woods grew thick, the meads a deeper hue;
The pipy summer growths swelled, lush and tall;
The sharp scythes swept at daybreak through the dew.
Thou didst not heed at all,
Thy prodigal voice grew dumb;
No more with song mightst thou beguile,
She sitting on her speckled eggs the while,
Thy mate's long vigil as the slow days went,
Solacing her with lays of measureless content.

Nay, nay, thy voice was Duty's, nor would dare
Sing were Love fled, though still the world were fair ;
The summer waxed and waned, the nights grew cold,
The sheep were thick within the wattled fold,
The woods began to moan,
Dumb wert thou and alone ;
Yet now, when leaves are sere, thy ancient note
Comes low and halting from thy doubtful throat.
Oh, lonely loveless voice, what dost thou here
In the deep silence of the fading year ?

Thus do I read the answer of thy song :
" I sang when winds blew chilly all day long ;
I sang because hope came and joy was near,
I sang a little while, I made good cheer ;
In summer's cloudless day
My music died away ;
But now the hope and glory of the year
Are dead and gone, a little while I sing
Songs of regret for days no longer here,
And touched with presage of the far-off Spring."

Is this the meaning of thy note, fair bird ?
Or do we read into thy simple brain
Echoes of thoughts which human hearts have stirred,
High-soaring joy and melancholy pain ?

Nay, nay, that lingering note
Belated from thy throat—
"Regret," is what it sings, "regret, regret!
The dear days pass, but are not wholly gone.
In praise of those I let my song go on;
'Tis sweeter to remember than forget."

RICHARD WATSON DIXON

Born 1833

SONG

The feathers of the willow
Are half of them grown yellow
  Above the swelling stream;
And ragged are the bushes,
And rusty now the rushes,
  And wild the clouded gleam.

The thistle now is older,
His stalks begin to moulder,
  His head is white as snow;
The branches all are barer,
The linnet's song is rarer,
  The robin pipeth now.

From "CHRIST'S COMPANY"

THE HOLY MOTHER AT THE CROSS

Of Mary's pains may now learn whoso will,
   When she stood underneath the groaning tree
Round which the true Vine clung: three hours the mill
   Of hours rolled round; she saw in visions three
The shadows walking underneath the sun,
   And these seemed all so very faint to be,
That she could scarcely tell how each begun,
   And went its way, minuting each degree
That it existed on the dial stone:
   For drop by drop of wine unfalteringly,
Not stroke by stroke in blood, the three hours gone
   She seemed to see.

Three hours she stood beneath the cross; it seemed
   To be a wondrous dial stone, for while
Upon the two long arms the sunbeams teemed,
   So was the head-piece like a centre stile;
Like to the dial where the judges sat
   Upon the grades, and the king crowned the pile,
In Zion town, that most miraculous plat
   On which the shadow backward did defile;
And now towards the third hour the sun enorme
   Dressed up all shadow to a bickering smile

I' the heat, and in its midst the form of form
  Lay like an isle.

Because that time so heavily beat and slow
  That fancy in each beat was come and gone;
Because that light went singing to and fro,
  A blissful song in every beam that shone;
Because that on the flesh a little tongue
  Instantly played, and spake in lurid tone;
Because that saintly shapes with harp and gong
  Told the three hours, whose telling made them one;
Half hid, involved in alternating beams,
  Half mute, they held the plectrum to the zone,
Therefore, as God her senses shield, it seems
  A dial stone.

Three hours she stood beside the cross; it seemed
  A splendid flower; for red dews on the edge
Stood dropping; petals doubly four she deemed
  Shot out like steel knives from the central wedge,
Which quadranted their perfect circle so
  As if four anthers should a vast flower hedge
Into four parts, and in its bosom, lo,
  The form lay, as the seed-heart holding pledge
Of future flowers; yea, in the midst was borne
  The head low drooped upon the swollen ledge
Of the torn breast; there was the ring of thorn
  This flower was fledge.

Because her woe stood all about her now,
　　No longer like a stream as ran the hour;
Because her cleft heart parted into two,
　　No more a mill-wheel spinning to time's power;
Because all motion seemed to be suspense;
　　Because one ray did other rays devour;
Because the sum of things rose o'er her sense,
　　She standing 'neath its dome as in a bower;
Because from one thing all things seemed to spume,
　　As from one mouth the fountain's hollow shower;
Therefore it seemed His and her own heart's bloom,
　　A splendid flower.

Now it was finished; shrivelled were the leaves
　　Of that pain-flower, and wasted all its bloom,
She felt what she had felt then; as receives,
　　When heaven is capable, the cloudy stroom
The edge of the white garment of the moon;
　　So felt she that she had received that doom;
And as an outer circle spins in tune,
　　Born of the inner on the sky's wide room,
Thinner and wider, that doom's memories,
　　Broken and thin and wild, began to come
As soon as this: St. John unwrapt his eyes,
　　And led her home.

WILLIAM MORRIS

Born 1834

THE CHAPEL IN LYONESS

SIR OZANA LE CURE HARDY. SIR GALAHAD. SIR BORS
DE GANYS

SIR OZANA

All day long and every day,
From Christmas-Eve to Whit-Sunday,
Within that Chapel-aisle I lay,
   And no man came a-near.

Naked to the waist was I,
And deep within my breast did lie,
Though no man any blood could spy,
   The truncheon of a spear.

No meat did ever pass my lips.
Those days—(Alas! the sunlight slips
From off the gilded parclose, dips,
   And night comes on apace.)

My arms lay back behind my head;
Over my raised-up knees was spread
A samite cloth of white and red;
   A rose lay on my face.

Many a time I tried to shout;
But as in dream of battle-rout,
My frozen speech would not well out;
   I could not even weep.

With inward sigh I see the sun
Fade off the pillars one by one,
My heart faints when the day is done,
   Because I cannot sleep.

Sometimes strange thoughts pass through my
      head;
Not like a tomb is this my bed,
Yet oft I think that I am dead;
   That round my tomb is writ,

"Ozana of the hardy heart,
   Knight of the Table Round,
Pray for his soul, lords, of your part;
   A true knight he was found."
Ah! me, I cannot fathom it.

                            He sleeps.

WILLIAM MORRIS

SIR GALAHAD

All day long and every day,
Till his madness pass'd away,
I watch'd Ozana as he lay
   Within the gilded screen.

All my singing moved him not;
As I sung my heart grew hot,
With the thought of Launcelot
   Far away, I ween.

So I went a little space
From out the chapel, bathed my face
In the stream that runs apace
   By the churchyard wall.

There I pluck'd a faint wild rose,
Hard by where the linden grows,
Sighing over silver rows
   Of the lilies tall.

I laid the flower across his mouth;
The sparkling drops seem'd good for drouth;
He smiled, turn'd round towards the south,
   Held up a golden tress.

The light smote on it from the west:
He drew the covering from his breast,
Against his heart that hair he prest;
    Death him soon will bless.

SIR BORS

I enter'd by the western door;
    I saw a knight's helm lying there:
I raised my eyes from off the floor,
    And caught the gleaming of his hair.

I stept full softly up to him;
    I laid my chin upon his head;
I felt him smile; my eyes did swim,
    I was so glad he was not dead.

I heard Ozana murmur low,
    "There comes no sleep nor any love."
But Galahad stoop'd and kiss'd his brow:
    He shiver'd; I saw his pale lips move.

SIR OZANA

There comes no sleep nor any love;
    Ah me! I shiver with delight.

I am so weak I cannot move;
  God move me to thee, dear, to-night!
Christ help! I have but little wit:
  My life went wrong; I see it writ,

"Ozana of the hardy heart,
  Knight of the Table Round,
Pray for his soul, lords, on your part,
  A good knight he was found."
Now I begin to fathom it.
                       He dies.

SIR BORS

Galahad sits dreamily;
What strange things may his eyes see,
Great blue eyes fix'd full on me?
On his soul, Lord, have mercy.

SIR GALAHAD

Ozana, shall I pray for thee?
  Her cheek is laid to thine;
No long time hence, also I see
  Thy wasted fingers twine

Within the tresses of her hair
  That shineth gloriously,
Thinly outspread in the clear air
  Against the jasper sea.

THE HAYSTACK IN THE FLOODS

Had she come all the way for this,
To part at last without a kiss?
Yea, had she borne the dirt and rain
That her own eyes might see him slain
Beside the haystack in the floods?

Along the dripping leafless woods,
The stirrup touching either shoe,
She rode astride as troopers do;
With kirtle kilted to her knee,
To which the mud splash'd wretchedly;
And the wet dripp'd from every tree
Upon her head and heavy hair,
And on her eyelids broad and fair;
The tears and rain ran down her face.
By fits and starts they rode apace,
And very often was his place
Far off from her; he had to ride
Ahead, to see what might betide
When the roads cross'd; and sometimes, when
There rose a murmuring from his men,
Had to turn back with promises;
Ah me! she had but little ease;

And often for pure doubt and dread
She sobb'd, made giddy in the head
By the swift riding; while, for cold,
Her slender fingers scarce could hold
The wet reins; yea, and scarcely, too,
She felt the foot within her shoe
Against the stirrup; all for this,
To part at last without a kiss
Beside the haystack in the floods.

For when they near'd that old soak'd hay,
They saw across the only way
That Judas, Godmar, and the three
Red running lions dismally
Grinn'd from his pennon, under which,
In one straight line along the ditch,
They counted thirty heads.

                    So then,
While Robert turn'd round to his men,
She saw at once the wretched end,
And, stooping down, tried hard to rend
Her coif the wrong way from her head,
And hid her eyes; while Robert said:
"Nay, love, 'tis scarcely two to one,
At Poictiers where we made them run
So fast—why, sweet my love, good cheer,

The Gascon frontier is so near,
Nought after this."

                    But, "O," she said,
"My God! My God! I have to tread
The long way back without you ; then
The court at Paris ; those six men ;
The gratings of the Chatelet ;
The swift Seine on some rainy day
Like this, and people standing by,
And laughing, while my weak hands try
To recollect how strong men swim.
All this, or else a life with him,
For which I should be damned at last,
Would God that this next hour were past!"

He answer'd not, but cried his cry,
"St. George for Marny!" cheerily ;
And laid his hand upon her rein.
Alas ! no man of all his train
Gave back that cheery cry again ;
And, while for rage his thumb beat fast
Upon his sword-hilts, some one cast
About his neck a kerchief long,
And bound him.

                  Then they went along

To Godmar; who said: "Now, Jehane,
Your lover's life is on the wane
So fast, that, if this very hour
You yield not as my paramour,
He will not see the rain leave off—
Nay, keep your tongue from gibe and scoff,
Sir Robert, or I slay you now."

She laid her hand upon her brow,
Then gazed upon the palm, as though
She thought her forehead bled, and—"No."
She said, and turn'd her head away,
As there were nothing else to say,
And everything were settled: red
Grew Godmar's face from chin to head:
"Jehane, on yonder hill there stands
My castle, guarding well my lands:
What hinders me from taking you,
And doing that I list to do
To your fair wilful body, while
Your knight lies dead?"

                      A wicked smile
Wrinkled her face, her lips grew thin,
A long way out she thrust her chin:
"You know that I should strangle you
While you were sleeping; or bite through

Your throat, by God's help—ah!" she said,
"Lord Jesus, pity your poor maid!
For in such wise they hem me in,
I cannot choose but sin and sin,
Whatever happens: yet I think
They could not make me eat or drink,
And so should I just reach my rest."
"Nay, if you do not my behest,
O Jehane! though I love you well,"
Said Godmar, "would I fail to tell
All that I know." "Foul lies," she said.
"Eh? lies my Jehane? By God's head,
At Paris folks would deem them true!
Do you know, Jehane, they cry for you,
'Jehane the brown! Jehane the brown!
Give us Jehane to burn or drown!'—
Eh—gag me, Robert!—sweet my friend,
This were indeed a piteous end
For those long fingers, and long feet,
And long neck, and smooth shoulders sweet;
An end that few men would forget
That saw it—So, an hour yet:
Consider, Jehane, which to take
Of life or death!"

     So, scarce awake,
Dismounting, did she leave that place,

And totter some yards : with her face
Turn'd upward to the sky she lay,
Her head on a wet heap of hay,
And fell asleep ; and while she slept,
And did not dream, the minutes crept
Round to the twelve again ; but she,
Being waked at last, sigh'd quietly,
And strangely childlike came, and said :
" I will not." Straightway Godmar's head,
As though it hung on strong wires, turn'd
Most sharply round, and his face burn'd.

For Robert—both his eyes were dry,
He could not weep, but gloomily
He seem'd to watch the rain ; yea, too,
His lips were firm ; he tried once more
To touch her lips ; she reach'd out, sore
And vain desire so tortured them,
The poor grey lips, and now the hem
Of his sleeve brush'd them.

                                              With a start
Up Godmar rose, thrust them apart ;
From Robert's throat he loosed the bands
Of silk and mail ; with empty hands
Held out, she stood and gazed, and saw,
The long bright blade without a flaw

Glide out from Godmar's sheath, his hand
In Robert's hair; she saw him bend
Back Robert's head; she saw him send
The thin steel down; the blow told well,
Right backward the knight Robert fell,
And moan'd as dogs do, being half dead,
Unwitting, as I deem: so then
Godmar turn'd grinning to his men,
Who ran, some five or six, and beat
His head to pieces at their feet.

Then Godmar turn'd again and said:
"So, Jehane, the first fitte is read!
Take note, my lady, that your way
Lies backward to the Chatelet!"
She shook her head and gazed awhile
At her cold hands with a rueful smile,
As though this thing had made her mad.

This was the parting that they had
Beside the haystack in the floods.

From "THE LIFE AND DEATH OF JASON"

I

Now Neptune, joyful of the sacrifice
Beside the sea, and all the gifts of price
That Jason gave him, sent them wind at will,
And swiftly Argo climbed each changing hill,
And ran through rippling valleys of the sea;
Nor toiled the heroes unmelodiously,
For by the mast sat great Œager's son,
And through the harp-strings let his fingers run
Nigh soundless, and with closed lips for a while;
But soon across his face there came a smile,
And his glad voice brake into such a song
That swiftlier sped the eager ship away.

"O bitter sea, tumultuous sea,
Full many an ill is wrought by thee!—
Unto the wasters of the land
Thou holdest out thy wrinkled hand;
And when they leave the conquered town,
Whose black smoke makes thy surges brown,
Driven betwixt thee and the sun,
As the long day of blood is done,

From many a league of glittering waves
Thou smilest on them and their slaves.
" The thin bright-eyed Phœnician
Thou drawest to thy waters wan,
With ruddy eve and golden morn
Thou temptest him, until, forlorn,
Unburied, under alien skies
Cast up ashore his body lies.
" Yea, whoso sees thee from his door,
Must ever long for more and more ;
Nor will the beechen bowl suffice,
Or homespun robe of little price,
Or hood well-woven from the fleece
Undyed, or unspiced wine of Greece ;
So sore his heart is set upon
Purple, and gold, and cinnamon ;
For as thou cravest, so he craves,
Until he rolls beneath thy waves.
Nor in some landlocked, unknown bay,
Can satiate thee for one day.

" Now, therefore, O thou bitter sea,
With no long words we pray to thee,
But ask thee, hast thou felt before
Such strokes of the long ashen oar ?
And hast thou yet seen such a prow
Thy rich and niggard waters plough ?

"Nor yet, O sea, shalt thou be cursed,
If at thy hands we gain the worst,
And, wrapt in water, roll about
Blind-eyed, unheeding song or shout,
Within thine eddies far from shore.
Warmed by no sunlight any more.

"Therefore, indeed, we joy in thee,
And praise thy greatness, and will we
Take at thy hands both good and ill,
Yea, what thou wilt, and praise thee still,
Enduring not to sit at home,
And wait until the last days come,
When we no more may care to hold
White bosoms under crowns of gold,
And our dulled hearts no longer are
Stirred by the clangorous noise of war,
And hope within our souls is dead,
And no joy is remembered.

"So, if thou hast a mind to slay,
Fair prize thou hast of us to-day;
And if thou hast a mind to save,
Great praise and honour shalt thou have;
But whatso thou wilt do with us,
Our end shall not be piteous,
Because our memories shall live
When folk forget the way to drive

The black keel through the heaped-up sea,
And half dried up by waters be."

II

SONG

"I know a little garden close
Set thick with lily and red rose,
Where I would wander if I might
From dewy dawn to dewy night,
And have one with me wandering.

"And though within it no birds sing,
And though no pillared house is there,
And though the apple boughs are bare
Of fruit and blossom, would to God,
Her feet upon the green grass trod,
And I beheld them as before.

"There comes a murmur from the shore,
And in the place two fair streams are,
Drawn from the purple hills afar,
Drawn down unto the restless sea;
The hills whose flowers ne'er fed the bee,
The shore no ship hath ever seen,
Still beaten by the billows green,
Whose murmur comes unceasingly
Unto the place for which I cry.

"For which I cry both day and night,
For which I let slip all delight,
That maketh me both deaf and blind,
Careless to win, unskilled to find,
And quick to lose what all men seek.

"Yet tottering as I am, and weak,
Still have I left a little breath
To seek within the jaws of death
An entrance to that happy place,
To seek the unforgotten face
Once seen, once kissed, once reft from me
Anigh the murmuring of the sea."

From "THE EARTHLY PARADISE"

INTRODUCTION

Of Heaven or Hell I have no power to sing,
I cannot ease the burden of your fears,
Or make quick-coming death a little thing,
Or bring again the pleasure of past years,
Nor for my words shall ye forget your tears,
Or hope again for aught that I can say,
The idle singer of an empty day.

But rather, when aweary of your mirth,
From full hearts still unsatisfied ye sigh,
And, feeling kindly unto all the earth,
Grudge every minute as it passes by,
Made the more mindful that the sweet days die—
—Remember me a little then I pray,
The idle singer of an empty day.

The heavy trouble, the bewildering care
That weighs us down who live and earn our bread,
These idle verses have no power to bear;
So let me sing of names remembered,
Because they, living not, can ne'er be dead,
Or long time take their memory quite away
From us poor singers of an empty day.

Dreamer of dreams, born out of my due time,
Why should I strive to set the crooked straight?
Let it suffice me that my murmuring rhyme
Beats with light wing against the ivory gate,
Telling a tale not too importunate
To those who in the sleepy region stay,
Lulled by the singer of an empty day.

Folk say, a wizard to a northern king
At Christmas-tide such wondrous things did show,
That through one window men beheld the spring,

And through another saw the summer glow,
And through a third the fruited vines a-row,
While still, unheard, but in its wonted way,
Piped the drear wind of that December day.

  So with this Earthly Paradise it is,
If ye will read aright, and pardon me,
Who strive to build a shadowy isle of bliss
Midmost the beating of the steely sea,
Where tossed about all hearts of men must be;
Whose ravening monsters mighty men shall slay,
Not the poor singer of an empty day.

From "LOVE IS ENOUGH"

THE MUSIC

Love is enough: ho ye who seek saving,
  Go no further; come hither; there have been who
    have found it,
And these know the House of Fulfilment of Craving;
  These know the Cup with the roses around it;
  These know the World's Wound and the balm that
    hath bound it:
Cry out, the World heedeth not, 'Love, lead us
  home!'

He leadeth, He hearkeneth, He cometh to you-ward;
  Set your faces as steel to the fears that assemble
Round his goad for the faint, and his scourge for the
    froward:
  Lo his lips, how with tales of last kisses they
    tremble!
  Lo his eyes of all sorrow that may not dissemble!
Cry out, for he heedeth, 'O Love, lead us home!'

O hearken the words of his voice of compassion:
  'Come cling round about me, ye faithful who sicken
Of the weary unrest and the world's passing fashion!
  As the rain in mid-morning your troubles shall
    thicken,
  But surely within you some Godhead doth quicken,
As ye cry to me heeding, and leading you home.

'Come—pain ye shall have, and be blind to the
    ending!
  Come—fear ye shall have, mid the sky's overcasting!
Come—change ye shall have, for far are ye wending!
  Come—no crown ye shall have for your thirst and
    your fasting,
  But the kissed lips of Love and fair life everlasting!
Cry out, for one heedeth, who leadeth you home!'

Is he gone? was he with us?—ho ye who seek saving,
  Go no further; come hither; for have we not found it?

Here is the House of Fulfilment of Craving;
  Here is the Cup with the roses around it;
    The World's Wound well healed, and the balm that
      hath bound it:
Cry out! for he heedeth, fair Love that led home.

THE MESSAGE OF THE MARCH WIND

Fair now is the spring-tide, now earth lies beholding
With the eyes of a lover, the face of the sun;
Long lasteth the daylight, and hope is enfolding
The green-growing acres with increase begun.

Now sweet, sweet it is through the land to be straying,
'Mid the birds and the blossoms and the beasts of the
    field;
Love mingles with love, and no evil is weighing
On thy heart or mine, where all sorrow is healed.

From township to township, o'er down and by tillage,
Far, far have we wandered and long was the day;
But now cometh eve at the end of the village,
Where over the grey wall the church riseth grey.

There is wind in the twilight; in the white road
    before us
The straw from the ox-yard is blowing about;
The moon's rim is rising, a star glitters o'er us,
And the vane on the spire-top is swinging in doubt.

Down there dips the highway, toward the bridge
    crossing over
The brook that runs on to the Thames and the sea.
Draw closer, my sweet, we are lover and lover;
This eve art thou given to gladness and me.

Shall we be glad always? Come closer and hearken:
Three fields further on, as they told me down there,
When the young moon has set, if the March sky
    should darken,
We might see from the hill-top the great city's glare.

Hark, the wind in the elm-boughs! from London it
    bloweth,
And telleth of gold, and of hope and unrest;
Of power that helps not; of wisdom that knoweth,
But teacheth not aught of the worst and the best.

Of the rich men it telleth, and strange is the story
How they have and they hanker, and grip far and
    wide;

And they live and they die, and the earth and its
    glory
Has been but a burden they scarce might abide.

Hark! the March wind again of a people is telling;
Of the life that they live there, so haggard and grim,
That if we and our love amidst them had been
    dwelling,
My fondness had faltered, thy beauty grown dim.

This land we have loved in our love and our leisure,
For them hangs in heaven, high out of their reach;
The wide hills o'er the sea-plain for them have no
    pleasure,
The grey homes of their fathers no story to teach.

The singers have sung and the builders have builded,
The painters have fashioned their tales of delight;
For what and for whom hath the world's book been
    gilded,
When all is for these but the blackness of night?

How long, and for what is their patience abiding?
How long and how oft shall their story be told,
While the hope that none seeketh in darkness is
    hiding,
And in grief and in sorrow the world groweth old?

Come back to the inn, love, and the lights and the fire,
And the fiddler's old tune and the shuffling of feet;
For there in a while shall be rest and desire,
And there shall the morrow's uprising be sweet.

Yet, love, as we wend, the wind bloweth behind us,
And beareth the last tale it telleth to-night,
How here in the spring-tide the message shall find us;
For the hope that none seeketh is coming to light.

Like the seed of midwinter, unheeded, unperished,
Like the autumn-sown wheat 'neath the snow lying green,
Like the love that o'ertook us, unawares and uncherished,
Like the babe 'neath thy girdle that groweth unseen;

So the hope of the people now buddeth and groweth,
Rest fadeth before it, and blindness and fear;
It biddeth us learn all the wisdom it knoweth;
It hath found us and held us, and biddeth us hear:

For it beareth the message: "Rise up on the morrow,
And go on thy ways toward the doubt and the strife;
Join hope to our hope and blend sorrow with sorrow,
And seek for men's love in the short days of life."

But lo, the old inn, and the lights, and the fire,
And the fiddler's old tune and the shuffling of feet;
Soon for us shall be quiet and rest and desire,
And to-morrow's uprising to deeds shall be sweet.

Then "Cuckoo! Cuck! Cuck! Cuck-oo!" he called,
  And he laughed and he chuckled cheerly;
"Your hearts they run dry and your heads grow bald,
  But I come back with April yearly.

"I come in the month that is sweet, so sweet,
  Though its sweetness be frail and fickle,
In the season when shower and sunshine meet,
  And you reck not of Autumn's sickle.

"I flout at the April loves of men
  And the kisses of trustful maidens;
And then I call 'Cuckoo!' again, again,
  With a jeering and jocund cadence.

"When the hawthorn blows and the yaffel mates,
  I sing and am silent never;
Just as love of itself in the May-time prates,
  As though it will last for ever!

"And in June, ere I go, I double the note,
  As I flit from cover to cover:
Are not vows, at the last, repeated by rote
  By fading and fleeting lover?"

A tear trickled down my true love's cheek
  At the words of the mocking rover;

She clung to my side, but she did not speak,
    And I kissed her over and over.

And while she leaned on my heart as though
    Her love in its depths was rooting,
There rose from the thicket behind us, slow,
    O such a silvery fluting!

When the long smooth note, as it seemed, must break,
    It fell in a swift sweet treble,
Like the sound that is made when a stream from a lake
    Gurgles o'er stone and pebble.

And I cried, "O nightingale! tell me true,
    Is your music rapture or weeping?
And why do you sing the whole night through,
    When the rest of the world is sleeping?"

Then it fluted: "My notes are of love's pure strain,
    And could there be descant fitter?
For why do you sever joy and pain,
    Since love is both sweet and bitter?

My song now wails of the sighs, the tears,
    The long absence that makes love languish;
Then thrills with its fluttering hopes and fears,
    Its rapture,—again its anguish.

"And why should my notes be hushed at night?
  Why sing in the sunlight only?
Love loves when 'tis dark, as when 'tis bright,
  Nor ceaseth because 'tis lonely."

My love looked up with a happy smile,
  (For a moment the woods were soundless):
The smile of a heart that knows no guile,
  And whose trust is deep and boundless.

And as I smiled that her smile betrayed
  The fulness of love's surrender,
Came a note from the heart of the forest shade,
  O so soft, and smooth, and tender!

'Twas but one note, and it seemed to brood
  On its own sufficing sweetness;
That cooed, and cooed, and again but cooed
  In a round, selfsame completeness.

Then I said, "There is, ringdove, endless bliss
  In the sound that you keep renewing:
But have you no other note than this,
  And why are you always cooing?"

The ringdove answered: "I too descant
  Of love as the woods keep closing;

Not of springtime loves that exalt and pant,
  But of harvest love reposing.

" If I coo all day on the selfsame bough,
  While the noisy popinjay ranges,
'Tis that love which is mellow keeps its vow,
  And callow love shifts and changes.

" When summer shall silence the merle's loud throat
  And the nightingale's sweet sad singing,
You still will hear my contented note,
  On the branch where I now am clinging.

" For the rapture of fancy surely wanes,
  And anguish is lulled by reason ;
But the tender note of the heart remains
  Through all changes of leaf and season."

Then we plunged in the forest, my love and I,
  In the forest plunged deeper and deeper,
Till none could behold us save only the sky,
  Through a trellis of branch and creeper.

And we paired and nested away from sight
  In a bower of woodbine pearly ;
And she broods on our love from morn to night,
  And I sing to her late and early.

Nor till Death shall have stripped our lives as bare
    As the forest in wintry weather,
Will the world find the nest in the covert where
    We dwelt, loved, and sang together.

A MARCH MINSTREL

Hail! once again, that sweet strong note!
    Loud on my loftiest larch,
Thou quaverest with thy mottled throat,
    Brave minstrel of bleak March!

Hearing thee flute, who pines or grieves
    For vernal smiles and showers?
Thy voice is greener than the leaves,
    And fresher than the flowers.

Scorning to wait for tuneful May
    When every throat can sing,
Thou floutest Winter with thy lay,
    And art thyself the Spring.

While daffodils, half mournful still,
    Muffle their golden bells,
Thy silvery peal o'er landscape chill
    Surges, and sinks, and swells.

Across the unsheltered pasture floats
  The young lamb's shivering bleat:
There is no trembling in thy notes,
  For all the snow and sleet.

Let the bullace bide till frosts have ceased,
  The blackthorn loiter long;
Undaunted by the blustering east,
  Thou burgeonest into song.

Yet who can wonder thou dost dare
  Confront what others flee?
Thy carol cuts the keen March air
  Keener than it cuts Thee.

The selfish cuckoo tarrieth till
  April repays his boast.
Thou, thou art lavish of thy trill,
  Now when we need it most.

The nightingale, while buds are coy,
  Delays to chant its grief.
Brave throstle! thou dost pipe for joy,
  With never a bough in leaf.

Even fond turtle-doves forbear
  To coo till woods are warm:

Thou hast the heart to love and pair
  Ere the cherry blossoms swarm.

The skylark, fluttering to be heard
  In realms beyond his birth,
Soars vainly heavenward. Thou, wise bird!
  Art satisfied with earth.

Thy home is not upon the ground,
  Thy hope not in the sky:
Near to thy nest thy notes resound,
  Neither too low nor high.

Blow what wind will, thou dost rejoice
  To carol, and build, and woo.
Throstle! to me impart thy voice;
  Impart thy wisdom too!

PRIMROSES

I

Latest, earliest of the year,
Primroses that still were here,
Snugly nestling round the boles
Of the cut down chestnut poles,

When December's tottering tread
Rustled 'mong the deep leaves dead,
And with confident young faces
Peeped from out the sheltered places
When pale January lay
In its cradle day by day,
Dead or living, hard to say;
Now that mid-March blows and blusters,
Out you steal in tufts and clusters,
Making leafless lane and wood
Vernal with your hardihood.
Other lovely things are rare,
You are prodigal as fair.
First you come by ones and ones,
Lastly in battalions,
Skirmish along hedge and bank,
Turn old Winter's wavering flank,
Round his flying footsteps hover,
Seize on hollow, ridge and cover,
Leave nor slope nor hill unharried,
Till, his snowy trenches carried,
O'er his sepulchre you laugh,
Winter's joyous epitaph.

II

This, too, be your glory great,
Primroses, you do not wait,

As the other flowers do,
For the Spring to smile on you,
But with coming are content,
Asking no encouragement.
Ere the hardy crocus cleaves
Sunny borders 'neath the eaves,
Ere the thrush his song rehearse
Sweeter than all poet's verse,
Ere the early bleating lambs
Cling like shadows to their dams,
Ere the blackthorn breaks to white,
Snowy-hooded anchorite;
Out from every hedge you look,
You are bright by every brook,
Wearing for your sole defence
Fearlessness of innocence.
While the daffodils still waver,
Ere the jonquil gets its savour,
While the linnets yet but pair,
You are fledged, and everywhere.
Nought can daunt you, nought distress,
Neither cold nor sunlessness.
You, when Lent sleet flies apace,
Look the tempest in the face;
As descend the flakes more slow,
From your eyelids shake the snow,
And when all the clouds have flown,

Meet the sun's smile with your own.
Nothing ever makes you less
Gracious to ungraciousness.
March may bluster up and down,
Pettish April sulk and frown;
Closer to their skirts you cling,
Coaxing Winter to be Spring.

III

Then when your sweet task is done,
And the wild flowers, one by one,
Here, there, everywhere do blow,
Primroses, you haste to go,
Satisfied with what you bring,
Fading morning-stars of Spring.
You have brightened doubtful days,
You have sweetened long delays,
Fooling our enchanted reason
To miscalculate the season.
But when doubt and fear are fled,
When the kine leave wintry shed,
And 'mid grasses green and tall
Find their fodder, make their stall;
When the wintering swallow flies
Homeward back from southern skies,
To the dear old cottage thatch
Where it loves to build and hatch,

That its young may understand,
Nor forget, this English land;
When the cuckoo, mocking rover,
Laughs that April loves are over;
When the hawthorn, all ablow,
Mimics the defeated snow;
Then you give one last look round;
Stir the sleepers under ground,
Call the campion to awake,
Tell the speedwell courage take,
Bid the eyebright have no fear,
Whisper in the bluebell's ear
Time has come for it to flood
With its blue waves all the wood,
Mind the stichwort of its pledge
To replace you in the hedge,
Bid the ladysmocks good-bye,
Close your bonnie lids and die;
And, without one look of blame,
Go as gently as you came.

TO ENGLAND

Men deemed thee fallen, did they? fallen like Rome
Coiled into self to foil a Vandal throng:
Not wholly shorn of strength, but vainly strong;
Weaned from thy fame by a too happy home,
Scanning the ridges of thy teeming loam,
Counting thy flocks, humming thy harvest song,
Callous, because thyself secure, 'gainst wrong,
Behind the impassable fences of the foam!
The dupes! Thou dost but stand erect, and lo!
The nations cluster round; and while the horde
Of wolfish backs slouch homeward to their snow,
Thou, 'mid thy sheaves in peaceful seasons stored,
Towerest supreme, victor without a blow,
Smilingly leaning on thy undrawn sword!

SIR ALFRED LYALL

Born 1835

A RAJPOOT CHIEF OF THE OLD SCHOOL

MORIBUNDUS LOQUITUR

And why say ye that I must leave
  This pleasure-garden, where the sun
Is baffled by the boughs that weave
  Their shade o'er my pavilion?
The trees I planted with my hands,
This house I built among the sands,
  Within a lofty wall which rounds
    This green oasis, kept with care;
  With room for my horses, hawks and hounds,
    And the cool arcade for my ladies fair.

How often, while the landscape flames
  With heat, within the marble court
I lie, and laugh to see my dames
  About the shimmering fountain sport:
Or after the long scorching days,
When the hot wind hushes, and falling, stays
  The clouds of dust, and stars are bright,
    I've spread my carpets in the grove,

And talked and loitered the live-long night
  With some foreign leman light o'love.

My wives—I married, as was fit,
  Some thirteen of the purest blood—
And two or three have germs of wit,
  And almost all are chaste and good;
But all their womanhood has been
Hencooped behind a marble screen;
  They count their pearls and doze—while she,
    The courtezan, had travelled far,
  Her songs were fresh, her talk was free
    Of the Delhi Court, or the Kábul War.

Those days are gone, I am old and ill,
  Why should I move? I love the place;
The dawn is fresh, the nights are still;
  Ah yes! I see it in your face,
My latest dawn and night are nigh,
And of my clan a chief must die
  Within the ancestral rampart's fold
    Paced by the listening sentinel,
  Where ancient cannon, and beldames old
    As the guns, peer down from the citadel.

Once more, once only, they shall bear
  My litter up the steep ascent

That pierces, mounting stair on stair,
  The inmost ring of battlement.
Oft-times that frowning gate I've past
(This time, but one, shall be the last)
  Where the tribal demon's image stands
    Crowning the arch, and on the side
  Are scarlet prints of woman's hands—
    Farewell! and forth must the lady ride,

Her face unveiled, in rich attire,
  She strikes the stone with fingers red,
" Farewell the palace, to the pyre
  We follow, widows of the dead!"
And I, whose life has reached its verge,
Bethink me of the wailing dirge
  That day my father forth was borne
    High seated, swathed in many a shawl,
  By priests who scatter flowers, and mourn ;
    And the eddying smoke of the funeral.

Thus did he vanish ; with him went
  Seven women, by the flames set free ;
I built a stately monument
  To shrine their graven effigy :
In front my father, godlike, stands,
The widows kneel with folded hands ;

All yearly rites are duly paid,
    All round are planted sacred trees,
And the ghosts are soothed by the spreading shade,
    And lulled by the strain of their obsequies.

His days were troubled; his curse I earned
    Full often, ere he passed that arch,
My father, by his farms we burned,
    By raiding on the English march;
And then that summer I rebelled,
One fort we seized, and there we held
    Until my father's guns grew hot;
        But the floods and darkness veiled our flight,
    We rode their lines with never a shot,
        For the matches were moist in the rainy night.

That's forty years ago; and since,
    With all these wild unruly clans,
In this salt wilderness, a prince
    Of camel-riding caterans,
I've sought religiously, Heaven knows,
A life of worship and repose,
    Vext by the stiff ungrateful league
        Of all my folk in fretful stir,
    By priests and gods in dark intrigue,
        And the wasting curse of the sorcerer.

They say I seized their broad estates,
   Upbraid me with a kinsman's blood;
He led his bands before my gates,
   And then—it was an ancient feud;
But I must offer gifts, and pray
The Brahmin's stain be washed away.
   Saint and poisoner, fed with bribes,
     Deep versed in every traitorous plan—
   I told them only to kill the scribes,
     But my Afgháns hated the holy man.

Yes, peace is blessed, and prayer is good;
   My eldest son defied my power;
I lost his mother in the wood
   That hides my lonely hunting-tower:
She was a proud unbroken dame:
Like son, like mother, hard to tame
   Or tire—And so he took the bent,
     His mother's kinsfolk at his heel,
   With many a restless malcontent;
     There were some had ease, ere I sheathed my steel.

The English say I govern ill,
   That laws must silence spear and gun,
So may my peaceful subjects till;
   But peaceful subjects have I none.

I can but follow my father's rule,
I cannot learn in an English school;
   Yet the hard world softens, and change is best,
     My sons must leave the ancient ways,
   The folk are weary, the land shall rest,
     And the gods are kind, for I end my days.

Then carry me to my castle steep,
   Whose time is ending with its lord's:
Eight months my grandsire held the keep
   Against the fierce Maratha hordes;
It would not stand three winter suns
Before the shattering English guns;
   And so these rude old faithful stones,
     My father's haven in high war-tide,
   Must rive and moulder, as soon my bones
     Shall bleach on the holy river-side.

Years hence, when all the earth is calm,
   And forts are level, and foes agree,
Since feuds must end, to trade and farm,
   And toil, like oxen, patiently;
When this my garden-palace stands
A desert ruin, choked with sands,
   A broken well 'mid trees that fade,
     Some traveller still my name may bless,
   The chief long syne that left him shade
     And a water spring in the wilderness.

JOHN LEICESTER WARREN, LORD DE TABLEY

Born 1835

CIRCE

This the house of Circe, queen of charms—
A kind of beacon-cauldron poised on high,
Hooped round with ember-clasping iron bars,
Sways in her palace porch, and smoulderingly
Drips out in blots of fire and ruddy stars;
But out behind that trembling furnace air,
The lands are ripe and fair,
Hush are the hills and quiet to the eye.
The river's reach goes by
With lamb and holy tower and squares of corn,
And shelving interspace
Of holly bush and thorn
And hamlets happy in an Alpine morn,
And deep-bowered lanes with grace
Of woodbine newly born.
But inward o'er the hearth a torch-head stands
Inverted, slow green flames of fulvous hue,

Echoed in wave-like shadows over her.
A censer's swing-chain set in her fair hands
Dances up wreaths of intertwisted blue
In clouds of fragrant frankincense and myrrh.
A giant tulip head and two pale leaves
Grew in the midmost of her chamber there,
A flaunting bloom, naked and undivine,
Rigid and bare,
Gaunt as a tawny bond-girl born to shame,
With freckled cheeks and splotched side serpentine,
A gipsy among flowers,
Unmeet for bed or bowers,
Virginal where pure-handed damsels sleep:
Let it not breathe a common air with them,
Lest when the night is deep,
And all things have their quiet in the moon,
Some birth of poison from its leaning stem
Waft in between their slumber-parted lips,
And they cry out or swoon,
Deeming some vampire sips,
Where riper Love may come for nectar boon!

And near this tulip, reared across a loom,
Hung a fair web of tapestry half done,
Crowding with folds and fancies half the room:
Men eyed as gods and damsels still as stone,
Pressing their brows alone,

In amethystine robes,
Or reaching at the polished orchard globes,
Or rubbing parted love-lips on their rind,
While the wind
Sows with sere apple leaves their breast and hair.
And all the margin there
Was arabesqued and bordered intricate
With hairy spider things
That catch and clamber,
And salamander in his dripping cave
Satanic ebon-amber;
Blind worm, and asp, and eft of cumbrous gait,
And toads who love rank grasses near a grave,
And the great goblin moth, who bears
Between his wings the ruined eyes of death;
And the enamelled sails
Of butterflies, who watch the morning's breath.
And many an emerald lizard with quick ears
Asleep in rocky dales.
And for an outer fringe embroidered small,
A ring of many locusts, horny-coated,
A round of chirping tree-frogs merry-throated,
And sly, fat fishes sailing, watching all.

THE TWO OLD KINGS

In ruling well what guerdon? Life runs low,
As yonder lamp upon the hour-glass lies,
Waning and wasted. We are great and wise,
But Love is gone; and Silence seems to grow

Along the misty road where we must go.
From summits near the morning star's uprise,
Death comes, a shadow from the northern skies,
As, when all leaves are down, thence comes the snow.

Brother and king, we hold our last carouse.
One loving cup we drain and then farewell.
The night is spent. The crystal morning ray

Calls us, as soldiers laurelled on our brows,
To march undaunted, while the clarions swell,
Heroic hearts, upon our lonely way.

WALTER THEODORE WATTS

Born 1836

NATURA MALIGNA

The Lady of the Hills with crimes untold
   Followed my feet, with azure eyes of prey;
   By glacier-brink she stood,—by cataract-spray,—
When mists were dire, or avalanche-echoes rolled.
At night she glimmered in the death-wind cold,
   And if a foot-print shone at break of day,
   My flesh would quail but straight my soul would say:
" 'Tis hers whose hand God's mightier hand doth hold."

I trod her snow-bridge, for the moon was bright,
   Her icicle-arch across the sheer crevasse,
   When lo, she stood! . . . God made her let me pass
Then felled the bridge! . . . Oh, in the sallow light
Adown the chasm, I saw her cruel, white,
   And all my wondrous days as in a glass.

JOHN THE PILGRIM

(THE MIRAGE IN EGYPT)

Beneath the sand-storm John the Pilgrim prays;
   But when he rises, lo! an Eden smiles,
   Green leafy slopes, meadows of camomiles,
Claspt in a silvery river's winding maze:
"Water, water! Blessèd be God!" he says,
   And totters gasping toward those happy isles.
   Then all is fled! Over the sandy piles
The bald-eyed vultures come and stand at gaze.

"God heard me not," says he, "blessèd be God,"
   And dies. But as he nears the pearly strand,
   Heav'n's outer coast where waiting angels stand,
He looks below: "Farewell, thou hooded clod,
   Brown corpse the vultures tear on bloody sand,
God heard my prayer for life—blessèd be God!"

THE FIRST KISS

If only in dreams may Man be fully blest,
  Is heav'n a dream? Is she I claspt a dream?—
  Or stood she here even now where dew-drops gleam,
And miles of furze shine golden down the West?
I seem to clasp her still—still on my breast
  Her bosom beats,—I see the blue eyes beam:—
  I think she kissed these lips, for now they seem
Scarce mine: so hallow'd of the lips they press'd!

Yon thicket's breath—can that be eglantine?
  Those birds—can they be morning's choristers?
  Can this be earth? Can these be banks of furze?—
Like burning bushes fired of God they shine!
I seem to know them, though this body of mine
  Pass'd into spirit at the touch of hers!

ALGERNON CHARLES SWINBURNE

Born 1837

From "ATALANTA IN CALYDON"

CHORUS

When the hounds of spring are on winter's traces,
    The mother of months in meadow or plain
Fills the shadows and windy places
    With lisp of leaves and ripple of rain;
And the brown bright nightingale amorous
Is half assuaged for Itylus,
For the Thracian ships and the foreign faces,
    The tongueless vigil, and all the pain.

Come with bows bent and with emptying of quivers,
    Maiden most perfect, lady of light,
With a noise of winds and many rivers,
    With a clamour of waters, and with might;
Bind on thy sandals, O thou most fleet,
Over the splendour and speed of thy feet;
For the faint east quickens, the wan west shivers,
    Round the feet of the day and the feet of the night.

Where shall we find her, how shall we sing to her,
    Fold our hands round her knees, and cling?
O that man's heart were as fire and could spring to her
    Fire, or the strength of the streams that spring!
For the stars and the winds are unto her
As raiment, as songs of the harp-player;
For the risen stars and the fallen cling to her,
    And the south west-wind and the west-wind sing.

For winter's rains and ruins are over,
    And all the season of snows and sins;
The days dividing lover and lover,
    The light that loses, the night that wins;
And time remembered is grief forgotten,
And frosts are slain and flowers begotten,
And in green underwood and cover
    Blossom by blossom the spring begins.

The full streams feed on flower of rushes,
    Ripe grasses trammel a travelling foot,
The faint fresh flame of the young year flushes
    From leaf to flower and flower to fruit;
And fruit and leaf are as gold and fire,
And the oat is heard above the lyre,
And the hoofèd heel of a satyr crushes
    The chestnut-husk at the chestnut-root.

And Pan by noon and Bacchus by night,
   Fleeter of foot than the fleet-foot kid,
Follows with dancing and fills with delight
   The Mænad and the Bassarid;
And soft as lips that laugh and hide
The laughing leaves of the trees divide,
And screen from seeing and leave in sight
   The god pursuing, the maiden hid.

The ivy falls with the Bacchanal's hair
   Over her eyebrows hiding her eyes;
The wild vine slipping down leaves bare
   Her bright breast shortening into sighs;
The wild vine slips with the weight of its leaves,
But the berried ivy catches and cleaves
To the limbs that glitter, the feet that scare
   The wolf that follows, the fawn that flies.

IN MEMORY OF WALTER SAVAGE LANDOR

Back to the flower-town, side by side,
   The bright months bring,
New-born, the bridegroom and the bride,
   Freedom and spring.

The sweet land laughs from sea to sea,
    Filled full of sun;
All things come back to her, being free;
    All things but one.

In many a tender wheaten plot
    Flowers that were dead
Live, and old suns revive; but not
    That holier head.

By this white wandering waste of sea,
    Far north, I hear
One face shall never turn to me
    As once this year:

Shall never smile and turn and rest
    On mine as there,
Nor one most sacred hand be prest
    Upon my hair.

I came as one whose thoughts half linger,
    Half run before;
The youngest to the oldest singer
    That England bore.

I found him whom I shall not find
    Till all grief end,

In holiest age our mightest mind,
    Father and friend.

But thou, if anything endure,
    If hope there be,
O spirit that man's life left pure,
    Man's death set free,

Not with disdain of days that were
    Look earthward now;
Let dreams revive the reverend hair,
    The imperial brow;

Come back in sleep, for in the life
    Where thou art not
We find none like thee. Time and strife
    And the world's lot

Move thee no more; but love at least
    And reverent heart
May move thee, royal and released,
    Soul, as thou art.

And thou, his Florence, to thy trust
    Receive and keep,
Keep safe his dedicated dust,
    His sacred sleep.

So shall thy lovers, come from far,
   Mix with thy name
As morning-star with evening-star
   His faultless fame.

From "THE GARDEN OF PROSERPINE"

Pale, beyond porch and portal,
   Crowned with calm leaves, she stands
Who gathers all things mortal
   With cold immortal hands;
Her languid lips are sweeter
Than love's who fears to greet her
To men that mix and meet her
   From many times and lands.

She waits for each and other,
   She waits for all men born;
Forgets the earth her mother,
   The life of fruits and corn;
And spring and seed and swallow
Take wing for her and follow
Where summer song rings hollow
   And flowers are put to scorn.

There go the loves that wither,
   The old loves with wearier wings;

And all dead years draw thither,
  And all disastrous things;
Dead dreams of days forsaken,
Blind buds that snows have shaken,
Wild leaves that winds have taken,
  Red strays of ruined springs.

We are not sure of sorrow,
  And joy was never sure;
To-day will die to-morrow;
  Time stoops to no man's lure;
And love, grown faint and fretful,
With lips but half regretful
Sighs, and with eyes forgetful
  Weeps that no loves endure.

From too much love of living,
  From hope and fear set free,
We thank with brief thanksgiving
  Whatever gods may be
That no life lives for ever;
That dead men rise up never;
That even the weariest river
  Winds somewhere safe to sea.

Then star nor sun shall waken,
  Nor any change of light:

> Nor sound of waters shaken,
>   Nor any sound or sight:
> Nor wintry leaves nor vernal,
> Nor days nor things diurnal;
> Only the sleep eternal
>   In an eternal night.

THE SUNDEW

> A little marsh-plant, yellow green,
> And pricked at lip with tender red.
> Tread close, and either way you tread
> Some faint black water jets between
> Lest you should bruise the curious head.
>
> A live thing may be; who shall know?
> The summer knows and suffers it;
> For the cool moss is thick and sweet
> Each side, and saves the blossom so
> That it lives out the long June heat.
>
> The deep scent of the heather burns
> About it; breathless though it be,
> Bow down and worship; more than we

Is the least flower whose life returns,
Least weed renascent in the sea.

We are vexed and cumbered in earth's sight
With wants, with many memories;
These see their mother what she is,
Glad-growing, till August leave more bright
The apple-coloured cranberries.

Wind blows and bleaches the strong grass,
Blown all one way to shelter it
From trample of strayed kine, with feet
Felt heavier than the moorhen was,
Strayed up past patches of wild wheat.

You call it sundew: how it grows,
If with its colour it have breath,
If life taste sweet to it, if death
Pain its soft petal, no man knows:
Man has no sight or sense that saith.

My sundew, grown of gentle days,
In these green miles the spring begun
Thy growth ere April had half done
With the soft secret of her ways
Or June made ready for the sun.

O red-lipped mouth of marsh-flower,
I have a secret halved with thee.
The name that is love's name to me
Thou knowest, and the face of her
Who is my festival to see.

The hard sun, as thy petals knew,
Coloured the heavy moss-water:
Thou wert not worth green midsummer
Nor fit to live to August blue,
O sundew, not remembering her.

From PRELUDE to "SONGS BEFORE SUNRISE"

Play then and sing; we too have played,
We likewise, in that subtle shade.
   We too have twisted through our hair
   Such tendrils as the wild Loves wear,
And heard what mirth the Mænads made,
   Till the wind blew our garlands bare
And left their roses disarrayed,
   And smote the summer with strange air,
And disengirdled and discrowned
The limbs and locks that vine-wreaths bound.

We too have tracked by star-proof trees
The tempest of the Thyiades
   Scare the loud night on hills that hid
   The blood-feasts of the Bassarid,
Heard their song's iron cadences
   Fright the wolf hungering from the kid,
Outroar the lion-throated seas,
   Outchide the north-wind if it chid,
And hush the torrent-tongued ravines
With thunders of their tambourines.

But the fierce flute whose notes acclaim
Dim goddesses of fiery fame,
   Cymbal and clamorous kettledrum,
   Timbrels and tabrets, all are dumb
That turned the high chill air to flame;
   The singing tongues of fire are numb
That called on Cotys by her name
   Edonian, till they felt her come
And maddened, and her mystic face
Lightened along the streams of Thrace.

For Pleasure slumberless and pale,
And Passion with rejected veil,
   Pass, and the tempest-footed throng
   Of hours that follow them with song
Till their feet flag and voices fail,

And lips that were so loud so long
Learn silence, or a wearier wail ;
  So keen is change, and time so strong,
To weave the robes of life and rend
And weave again till life have end.

But weak is change, but strengthless time,
To take the light from heaven, or climb
  The hills of heaven with wasting feet.
  Songs they can stop that earth found meet,
But the stars keep their ageless rhyme ;
  Flowers they can slay that spring thought sweet,
But the stars keep their spring sublime ;
  Passions and pleasures can defeat,
Actions and agonies control,
And life, and death, but not the soul.

Because man's soul is man's God still,
What wind soever waft his will
  Across the waves of day and night
  To port or shipwreck, left or right,
By shores and shoals of good and ill ;
  And still its flame at mainmast height
Through the rent air that foam-flakes fill
  Sustains the indomitable light
Whence only man hath strength to steer
Or helm to handle without fear.

Save his own soul's light overhead,
None leads him, and none ever led,
   Across birth's hidden harbour-bar,
    Past youth where shoreward shallows are,
Through age that drives on toward the red
   Vast void of sunset hailed from far,
To the equal waters of the dead;
   Save his own soul he hath no star,
And sinks, except his own soul guide,
Helmless in middle turn of tide.

No blast of air or fire of sun
Puts out the light whereby we run
   With girdled loins our lamplit race,
    And each from each takes heart of grace
And spirit till his turn be done,
   And light of face from each man's face
In whom the light of trust is one ;
   Since only souls that keep their place
By their own light, and watch things roll,
And stand, have light for any soul.

A little time we gain from time
To set our seasons in some chime,
   For harsh or sweet or loud or low,
    With seasons played out long ago
And souls that in their time and prime

Took part with summer or with snow,
Lived abject lives out or sublime,
  And had their chance of seed to sow
For service or disservice done
To those days dead and this their son.

A little time that we may fill
Or with such good works or such ill
  As loose the bonds or make them strong
  Wherein all manhood suffers wrong.
By rose-hung river and light-foot rill
  There are who rest not; who think long
Till they discern as from a hill,
  At the sun's hour of morning song,
Known of souls only, and those souls free,
The sacred spaces of the sea.

From "MATER TRIUMPHALIS"

I do not bid thee spare me, O dreadful mother!
  I pray thee that thou spare not, of thy grace.
How were it with me then, if ever another
  Should come to stand before thee in this my place?

I am the trumpet at thy lips, thy clarion
  Full of thy cry, sonorous with thy breath;

The graves of souls born worms and creeds grown
    carrion
  Thy blast of judgment fills with fires of death.

Thou art the player whose organ-keys are thunders,
  And I beneath thy foot the pedal prest,
Thou art the ray whereat the rent night sunders,
  And I the cloudlet borne upon thy breast.

I shall burn up before thee, pass and perish,
  As haze in sunrise on the red sea-line;
But thou from dawn to sunsetting shalt cherish
  The thoughts that led and souls that lighted mine.

Reared between night and noon and truth and error,
  Each twilight-travelling bird that trills and screams
Sickens at midday, nor can face for terror
  The imperious heaven's inevitable extremes.

I have no spirit of skill with equal fingers
  At sign to sharpen or to slacken strings;
I keep no time of song with gold-perched singers
  And chirp of linnets on the wrists of kings.

I am thy storm-thrush of the days that darken,
  Thy petrel in the foam that bears thy bark
To port through night and tempest; if thou hearken,
  My voice is in thy heaven before the lark.

My song is in the mist that hides thy morning,
  My cry is up before the day for thee;
I have heard thee and beheld thee and give warning,
  Before thy wheels divide the sky and sea.

Birds shall wake with thee voiced and feathered fairer,
  To see in summer what I see in spring;
I have eyes and heart to endure thee, O thunder-bearer,
  And they shall be who shall have tongues to sing.

I have love at least, and have not fear, and part not
  From thine unnavigable and wingless way;
Thou tarriest, and I have not said thou art not,
  Nor all thy night long have denied thy day.

Darkness to daylight shall lift up thy pæan,
  Hill to hill thunder, vale cry back to vale,
With wind-notes as of eagles Æschylean,
  And Sappho singing in the nightingale.

Sung to by mighty sons of dawn and daughters,
  Of this night's songs thine ear shall keep but one,
That supreme song which shook the channelled waters,
  And called thee skyward as God calls the sun.

Come, though all heaven again be fire above thee;
  Though death before thee come to clear thy sky;
Let us but see in his thy face who love thee;
  Yea, though thou slay us, arise and let us die.

From "HERTHA"

    The tree many-rooted
      That swells to the sky
    With frondage red-fruited,
      The life-tree am I ;
In the buds of your lives is the sap of my leaves : ye shall live and not die.

    But the Gods of your fashion
      That take and that give,
    In their pity and passion
      That scourge and forgive,
They are worms that are bred in the bark that falls off; they shall die and not live.

    My own blood is what stanches
      The wounds in my bark ;
    Stars caught in my branches
      Make day of the dark,
And are worshipped as suns till the sunrise shall tread out their fires as a spark.

    Where dead ages hide under
      The live roots of the tree,

In my darkness the thunder
　Makes utterance of me;
In the clash of my boughs with each other ye hear the
　waves sound of the sea.

That noise is of Time,
　As his feathers are spread
And his feet set to climb
　Through the boughs overhead,
And my foliage rings round him and rustles, and
　branches are bent with his tread.

The storm-winds of ages
　Blow through me and cease,
The war-wind that rages,
　The spring-wind of peace,
Ere the breath of them roughen my tresses, ere one of
　my blossoms increase.

All sounds of all changes,
　All shadows and lights
On the world's mountain-ranges
　And stream-riven heights,
Whose tongue is the wind's tongue and language of
　storm-clouds on earth-shaking nights;

All forms of all faces,
　All works of all hands

In unsearchable places
   Of time-stricken lands,
All death and all life, and all reigns and all ruins, drop
   through me as sands.

   Though sore be my burden
      And more than ye know,
   And my growth have no guerdon
      But only to grow,
Yet I fail not of growing for lightnings above me or
   deathworms below.

   These too have their part in me,
      As I too in these ;
   Such fire is at heart in me,
      Such sap is this tree's,
Which hath in it all sounds and all secrets of infinite
   lands and of seas.

   In the spring-coloured hours
      When my mind was as May's,
   There brake forth of me flowers
      By centuries of days,
Strong blossoms with perfume of manhood, shot out
   from my spirit as rays.

   And the sound of them springing
      And smell of their shoots

Were as warmth and sweet singing
    And strength to my roots;
And the lives of my children made perfect with freedom of soul were my fruits.

A FORSAKEN GARDEN

In a coign of the cliff between lowland and highland,
    At the sea-down's edge between windward and lee,
Walled round with rocks as an inland island,
    The ghost of a garden fronts the sea.
A girdle of brushwood and thorn encloses
    The steep square slope of the blossomless bed
Where the weeds that grew green from the graves of
        its roses
            Now lie dead.

The fields fall southward, abrupt and broken,
    To the low last edge of the long lone land.
If a step should sound or a word be spoken,
    Would a ghost not rise at the strange guest's hand?
So long have the grey bare walks lain guestless,
    Through branches and briers if a man make way,
He shall find no life but the sea-wind's, restless
            Night and day.

The dense hard passage is blind and stifled
  That crawls by a track none turn to climb
To the strait waste place that the years have rifled
  Of all but the thorns that are touched not of time.
The thorns he spares when the rose is taken;
  The rocks are left when he wastes the plain.
The wind that wanders, the weeds wind-shaken,
      These remain.

Not a flower to be prest of the foot that falls not;
  As the heart of a dead man the seed-plots are dry;
From the thicket of thorns whence the nightingale calls not,
  Could she call, there were never a rose to reply.
Over the meadows that blossom and wither
  Rings but the note of a sea-bird's song;
Only the sun and the rain come hither
      All year long.

The sun burns sere and the rain dishevels
  One gaunt bleak blossom of scentless breath.
Only the wind here hovers and revels
  In a round where life seems barren as death.
Here there was laughing of old, there was weeping,
  Haply, of lovers none ever will know,
Whose eyes went seaward a hundred sleeping
      Years ago.

Heart handfast in heart as they stood, "Look thither,"
  Did he whisper? "Look forth from the flowers to
    the sea;
For the foam-flowers endure when the rose-blossoms
    wither,
  And men that love lightly may die—but we?"
And the same wind sang and the same waves whitened,
  And or ever the garden's last petals were shed,
In the lips that had whispered, the eyes that had
    lightened,
      Love was dead.

Or they loved their life through, and then went
    whither?
  And were one to the end—but what end who knows?
Love deep as the sea as a rose must wither,
  As the rose-red seaweed that mocks the rose.
Shall the dead take thought for the dead to love them?
  What love was ever as deep as a grave?
They are loveless now as the grass above them
      Or the wave.

All are at one now, roses and lovers,
  Not known of the cliffs and the fields and the sea.
Not a breath of the time that has been hovers
  In the air now soft with a summer to be.

Not a breath shall there sweeten the seasons hereafter
   Of the flowers or the lovers that laugh now or weep,
When as they that are free now of weeping and laughter
      We shall sleep.

Here death may deal not again for ever;
   Here change may come not till all change end.
From the graves they have made they shall rise up never,
   Who have left nought living to ravage and rend.
Earth, stones, and thorns of the wild ground growing,
   When the sun and the rain live, these shall be;
Till a last wind's breath upon all these blowing
      Roll the sea.

Till the slow sea rise and the sheer cliff crumble,
   Till terrace and meadow the deep gulfs drink,
Till the strength of the waves of the high tides humble
   The fields that lessen, the rocks that shrink,
Here now in his triumph where all things falter,
   Stretched out on the spoils that his own hand spread,
As a god self-slain on his own strange altar,
      Death lies dead.

WILFRID SCAWEN BLUNT

Born 1840

TO MANON

COMPARING HER TO A FALCON

Brave as a falcon and as merciless,
With bright eyes watching still the world, thy prey,
I saw thee pass in thy lone majesty,
Untamed, unmated, high above the press.
The dull crowd gazed at thee. It could not guess
The secret of thy proud aërial way,
Or read in thy mute face the soul which lay
A prisoner there in chains of tenderness.
—Lo, thou art captured. In my hand to-day
I hold thee, and awhile thou deignest to be
Pleased with my jesses. I would fain beguile
My foolish heart to think thou lovest me: See,
I dare not love thee quite. A little while
And thou shalt sail back heavenwards. Woe is me!

A FOREST IN BOSNIA

Spirit of Trajan! What a world is here.
What remnant of old Europe in this wood
Of life primæval rude as in the year
When thy first legions by the Danube stood.
These are the very Dacians they subdued,
Swineherds and shepherds clad in skins of deer
And fox and marten still, a bestial brood,
Than their own swine begotten swinelier.
The fair oak-forest, their first heritage,
Pastures them still, and still the hollow oak
Receives them in its bosom. Still o'erhead
Upon the stag-head tops, grown hoar with age,
Calm buzzards sit and ancient ravens croak,
And all with solemn life is tenanted.

LILAC AND GOLD AND GREEN

I

Lilac and gold and green!
  Those are the colours I love the best,
Spring's own raiment untouched and clean,
  When the world is awake and yet hardly dressed,

And the stranger sun, her bridegroom shy,
Looks at her bosom and wonders why
   She is so beautiful, he so blest.

II

Lilac and green and gold!
   Those were the colours you wore to-day.
Robed you were in them fold on fold,
   Clothed in the light of your love's delay.
And I held you thus in my arms, once only,
And wondered still, as you left me lonely,
   How the world's beauty was changed to grey.

III

Lilac and gold and green!
   I would die for the truth of those colours true:
Lilac for loyalty, gold for my queen,
   And green the faith of my love for you.
Here is a posy of all the three.
My heart is with it. So think of me,
   And our weeping skies shall once more be blue.

From "IN VINCULIS"

Behold the Court of Penance. Four gaunt walls
   Shutting out all things but the upper heaven.
Stone flags for floor, where daily from their stalls
   The human cattle in a circle driven
   Tread down their pathway to a mire uneven,
Pale-faced, sad-eyed, and mute as funerals.
   Woe to the wretch whose weakness unforgiven
Falters a moment in the track or falls.
Yet is there consolation. Overhead
   The pigeons build and the loud jackdaws talk,
And once in the wind's eye, like a ship moored,
   A sea-gull flew and I was comforted.
Even here the heavens declare thy glory, Lord,
   And the free firmament thy handiwork.

My prison has its pleasures. Every day
   At breakfast-time, spare meal of milk and bread,
Sparrows come trooping in familiar way
   With head aside beseeching to be fed.
   A spider too for me has spun her thread

Across the prison rules, and a brave mouse
   Watches in sympathy the warder's tread,
These two my fellow prisoners in the house.

But about dusk in the rooms opposite
   I see lamps lighted, and upon the blind
A shadow passes all the evening through.
   It is the gaoler's daughter fair and kind
And full of pity—so I image it—
Till the stars rise, and night begins anew.

AUSTIN DOBSON

Born 1840

A DEAD LETTER

"*A cœur blessé—l'ombre et le silence*"
                      H. DE BALZAC

I

I drew it from its china tomb;—
  It came out feebly scented
With some thin ghost of past perfume
  That dust and days had lent it.

An old, old letter,—folded still!
  To read with due composure,
I sought the sun-lit window-sill
  Above the grey enclosure,

That glimmering in the sultry haze,
  Faint-flowered, dimly shaded,
Slumbered like Goldsmith's Madam Blaize,
  Bedizened and brocaded.

A queer old place! You'd surely say
    Some tea-board garden-maker
Had planned it in Dutch William's day
    To please some florist Quaker,

So trim it was. The yew-trees still,
    With pious care perverted,
Grew in the same grim shapes; and still
    The lipless dolphin spurted;

Still in his wonted state abode
    The broken-nosed Apollo;
And still the cypress-arbour showed
    The same umbrageous hollow.

Only,—as fresh young Beauty gleams
    From coffee-coloured laces,—
So peeped from its old-fashioned dreams
    The fresher modern traces;

For idle mallet, hoop, and ball
    Upon the lawn were lying;
A magazine, a tumbled shawl,
    Round which the swifts were flying;

And, tossed beside the Guelder rose,
    A heap of rainbow knitting,

Where, blinking in her pleased repose,
    A Persian cat was sitting.

"A place to love in,—live,—for aye,
    If we two, like Tithonus,
Could find some God to stretch the grey,
    Scant life the Fates have thrown us;

"But now by steam we run our race,
    With buttoned heart and pocket;
Our Love's a gilded, surplus grace,—
    Just like an empty locket!

"'The time is out of joint.' Who will,
    May strive to make it better;
For me, this warm old window-sill,
    And this old dusty letter."

II

"Dear *John* (the letter ran), it can't, can't be,
    For Father's gone to *Chorley Fair* with *Sam*,
And Mother's storing Apples,—*Prue* and Me
    Up to our Elbows making Damson Jam:
But we shall meet before a Week is gone,—
'' Tis a long Lane that has no Turning,' *John!*

"Only till Sunday next, and then you'll wait
    Behind the White-Thorn, by the broken Stile—

We can go round and catch them at the Gate,
  All to Ourselves, for nearly one long Mile;
Dear *Prue* won't look, and Father he'll go on,
And Sam's two Eyes are all for *Cissy, John!*

"*John*, she's so smart,—with every Ribbon new,
  Flame-coloured Sack, and Crimson Padesoy;
As proud as proud; and has the Vapours too,
  Just like My Lady;—calls poor *Sam* a Boy,
And vows no Sweet-heart's worth the Thinking-on
Till he's past Thirty ... I know better, *John!*

"My Dear, I don't think that I thought of much
  Before we knew each other, I and you;
And now, why, *John*, your least, least Finger-touch,
  Gives me enough to think a Summer through.
See, for I send you Something! There, 'tis gone!
Look in this corner,—mind you find it, *John!*"

III

This was the matter of the note,—
  A long-forgot deposit,
Dropped in an Indian dragon's throat,
  Deep in a fragrant closet,

Piled with a dapper Dresden world,—
  Beaux, beauties, prayers, and posies,—

Bonzes with squat legs undercurled,
  And great jars filled with roses.

Ah, heart that wrote! Ah, lips that kissed!
  You had no thought or presage
Into what keeping you dismissed
  Your simple old-world message!

A reverent one. Though we to-day
  Distrust beliefs and powers,
The artless, ageless things you say
  Are fresh as May's own flowers,

Starring some pure primeval spring,
  Ere Gold had grown despotic,—
Ere Life was yet a selfish thing,
  Or Love a mere exotic!

I need not search too much to find
  Whose lot it was to send it,
That feel upon me yet the kind,
  Soft hand of her who penned it;

And see, through two score years of smoke,
  In by-gone, quaint apparel,
Shine from yon time-black Norway oak
  The face of Patience Caryl,—

The pale, smooth forehead, silver-tressed;
　　The grey gown, primly flowered;
The spotless, stately coif whose crest
　　Like Hector's horse-plume towered;

And still the sweet half-solemn look
　　Where some past thought was clinging,
As when one shuts a serious book
　　To hear the thrushes singing.

I kneel to you! Of those you were,
　　Whose kind old hearts grow mellow,—
Whose fair old faces grow more fair
　　As Point and Flanders yellow;

Whom some old store of garnered grief,
　　Their placid temples shading,
Crowns like a wreath of autumn leaf
　　With tender tints of fading.

Peace to your soul! You died unwed—
　　Despite this loving letter.
And what of John? The less that's said
　　Of John, I think, the better.

A GENTLEMAN OF THE OLD SCHOOL

He lived in that past Georgian day,
When men were less inclined to say
That "Time is Gold," and overlay
    With toil their pleasure;
He held some land, and dwelt thereon,—
Where, I forget,—the house is gone;
His christian name, I think, was John,—
    His surname, Leisure.

Reynolds has painted him,—a face
Filled with a fine, old-fashioned grace,
Fresh-coloured, frank, with ne'er a trace
    Of trouble shaded;
The eyes are blue, the hair is drest
In plainest way,—one hand is prest
Deep in a flapped canary vest,
    With buds brocaded.

He wears a brown old Brunswick coat,
With silver buttons,—round his throat,
A soft cravat;—in all you note
    An elder fashion,—

A strangeness, which, to us who shine
In shapely hats,—whose coats combine
All harmonies of hue and line,
    Inspires compassion.

He lived so long ago, you see!
Men were untravelled then, but we,
Like Ariel, post o'er land and sea
    With careless parting;
He found it quite enough for him
To smoke his pipe in "garden trim,"
And watch, about the fish-tank's brim,
    The swallows darting.

He liked the well-wheel's creaking tongue,—
He liked the thrush that stopped and sung,—
He liked the drone of flies among
    His netted peaches;
He liked to watch the sunlight fall
Athwart his ivied orchard-wall;
Or pause to catch the cuckoo's call
    Beyond the beeches.

His were the times of Paint and Patch,
And yet no Ranelagh could match
The sober doves that round his thatch
    Spread tails and sidled;

He liked their ruffling, puffed content,—
For him their drowsy wheelings meant
More than a Mall of Beaux that bent,
    Or Belles that bridled.

Not that, in truth, when life began
He shunned the flutter of the fan;
He too had maybe "pinked his man"
    In Beauty's quarrel;
But now his "fervent youth" had flown
Where lost things go, and he was grown
As staid and slow-paced as his own
    Old hunter, Sorrel.

Yet still he loved the chase, and held
That no composer's score excelled
The merry horn, when Sweetlip swelled
    Its jovial riot;
But most his measured words of praise
Caressed the angler's easy ways,—
His idly meditative days,—
    His rustic diet.

Not that his "meditating" rose
Beyond a sunny summer doze;
He never troubled his repose
    With fruitless prying;

But held, as law for high and low,
What God withholds no man can know,
And smiled away inquiry so,
        Without replying.

We read—alas, how much we read!—
The jumbled strifes of creed and creed
With endless controversies feed
        Our groaning tables;
His books—and they sufficed him—were
Cotton's "Montaigne," "The Grave" of Blair,
A "Walton"—much the worse for wear,
        And "Æsop's Fables."

One more,—"The Bible."   Not that he
Had searched its page as deep as we;
No sophistries could make him see
        Its slender credit;
It may be that he could not count
The sires and sons to Jesse's fount,—
He liked the "Sermon on the Mount,"—
        And more, he read it.

Once he had loved, but failed to wed,
A red-cheeked lass who long was dead;
His ways were far too slow, he said,
        To quite forget her;

And still when time had turned him gray,
The earliest hawthorn buds in May
Would find his lingering feet astray,
      Where first he met her.

"*In Cælo Quies*" heads the stone
On Leisure's grave,—now little known,
A tangle of wild-rose has grown
      So thick across it;
The "Benefactions" still declare
He left the clerk an elbow-chair,
And "12 Pence Yearly to Prepare
      A Christmas Posset."

Lie softly, Leisure! Doubtless you,
With too serene a conscience drew
Your easy breath, and slumbered through
      The gravest issue;
But we, to whom our age allows
Scarce space to wipe our weary brows,
Look down upon your narrow house,
      Old friend, and miss you!

A SONG OF THE FOUR SEASONS

    When Spring comes laughing
      By vale and hill,
    By wind-flower walking
      And daffodil,—
    Sing stars of morning,
      Sing morning skies,
    Sing blue of speedwell,—
      And my Love's eyes.

    When comes the Summer,
      Full-leaved and strong,
    And gay birds gossip
      The orchard long,—
    Sing hid, sweet honey
      That no bee sips;
    Sing red, red roses,—
      And my Love's lips.

    When Autumn scatters
      The leaves again,
    And piled sheaves bury
      The broad-wheeled wain,—

    Sing flutes of harvest
      Where men rejoice;
    Sing rounds of reapers,—
      And my Love's voice.

    But when comes Winter
      With hail and storm,
    And red fire roaring
      And ingle warm,—
    Sing first sad going
      Of friends that part;
    Then sing glad meeting,—
      And my Love's heart.

TO AN INTRUSIVE BUTTERFLY

"Kill not—for Pity's sake—and lest ye slay
The meanest thing upon its upward way."
                      Five Rules of Buddha.

I watch you through the garden walks,
    I watch you float between
The avenues of dahlia stalks,
    And flicker on the green;
You hover round the garden seat,
    You mount, you waver. Why,—

Why storm us in our still retreat,
  O saffron Butterfly!

Across the room in loops of flight
  I watch you wayward go;
Dance down a shaft of glancing light,
  Review my books a-row;
Before the bust you flaunt and flit
  Of "blind Mæonides"—
Ah, trifler, on his lips there lit
  Not butterflies, but bees!

You pause, you poise, you circle up
  Among my old Japan;
You find a comrade on a cup,
  A friend upon a fan;
You wind anon, a breathing-while,
  Around Amanda's brow;—
Dost dream her then, O Volatile!
  E'en such an one as thou?

Away! Her thoughts are not as thine.
  A sterner purpose fills
Her steadfast soul with deep design
  Of baby bows and frills;
What care hath she for worlds without,—
  What heed for yellow sun,

Whose endless hopes revolve about
   A planet, *ætat* One!

Away! Tempt not the best of wives:
   Let not thy garish wing
Come fluttering our Autumn lives
   With truant dreams of Spring!
Away! Re-seek thy "Flowery Land;"
   Be Buddha's law obeyed;
Lest Betty's undiscerning hand
   Should slay . . . a future PRAED!

THE POET AND THE CRITICS

If those who wield the Rod forget,
'Tis truly—*Quis custodiet?*

A certain Bard (as Bards will do)
Dressed up his Poems for Review.
His Type was plain, his Title clear;
His Frontispiece by Fourdrinier.
Moreover he had on the Back
A sort of sheepskin Zodiac;—
A Mask, a Harp, an Owl,—in fine
A neat and "classical" Design.

But the *in*-Side?—Well, good or bad,
The Inside was the best he had :
Much Memory,—more Imitation ;—
Some Accidents of Inspiration ;—
Some Essays in that finer Fashion
Where Fancy takes the place of Passion ;—
And some (of course) more roughly wrought
To catch the Advocates of Thought.

In the less-crowded Age of Anne,
Our Bard had been a favoured Man ;
Fortune, more chary with the Sickle
Had ranked him next to Garth or Tickell ;—
He might have even dared to hope
A Line's Malignity from Pope !
But now, when Folks are hard to please,
And Poets are as thick as—Peas,
The Fates are not so prone to flatter,
Unless, indeed, a Friend . . . No Matter.

The Book, then, had a minor Credit :
The Critics took, and doubtless read it.
Said A.—*These little Songs display
No lyric Gift ; but still a Ray,—
A Promise. They will do no harm.*
'Twas kindly, if not *very* warm.
Said B.—*The Author may, in time*

Acquire the Rudiments of Rhyme:
His Efforts now are scarcely Verse.
This, certainly, could not be worse.

Sorely discomfited, our Bard
Worked for another ten years—hard.
Meanwhile the World, unmoved, went on;
New stars shot up, shone out, were gone;
Before his second Volume came
His Critics had forgot his Name:
And who, forsooth, is bound to know
Each Laureate *in embryo!*
They tried and tested him, no less,—
The pure Assayers of the Press.
Said A.—*The Author, may in Time* . . .
Or much what B. had said of Rhyme.
Then B.—*These little Songs display* . . .
And so forth, in the sense of A.
Over the Bard I throw a Veil.

There is no Moral to this Tale.

A FANCY FROM FONTENELLE

"De mémoires de Rose on n'a point vu mourir le Jardinier."

The Rose in the garden slipped her bud,
And she laughed in the pride of her youthful blood,
As she thought of the Gardener standing by—
"He is old,—so old! And he soon must die!"

The full Rose waxed in the warm June air,
And she spread and spread till her heart lay bare;
And she laughed once more as she heard his tread—
"He is older now! He will soon be dead!"

But the breeze of the morning blew, and found
That the leaves of the blown Rose strewed the ground;
And he came at noon, that Gardener old,
And he raked them softly under the mould.

And I wove the thing to a random rhyme,
For the Rose is Beauty, the Gardener Time.

BEFORE SEDAN

"The dead hand clasped a letter."
Special Correspondence.

Here, in this leafy place,
 Quiet he lies,
Cold, with his sightless face
 Turned to the skies;
'Tis but another dead;
All you can say is said.

Carry his body hence,—
 Kings must have slaves;
Kings climb to eminence
 Over men's graves:
So this man's eye is dim;—
Throw the earth over him.

What was the white you touched,
 There, at his side?
Paper his hand had clutched
 Tight ere he died;—
Message or wish, may be;—
Smooth the folds out and see.

Hardly the worst of us
    Here could have smiled !—
Only the tremulous
    Words of a child ;—
Prattle, that has for stops
Just a few ruddy drops.

Look. She is sad to miss,
    Morning and night,
His—her dead father's—kiss ;
    Tries to be bright,
Good to mamma, and sweet.
That is all. "Marguerite."

Ah, if beside the dead
    Slumbered the pain !
Ah, if the hearts that bled
    Slept with the slain !
If the grief died ;—But no ;—
Death will not have it so.

THE LADIES OF ST. JAMES'S

The ladies of St. James's
    Go swinging to the play ;

Their footmen go before them,
  With a "Stand by! Clear the way!"
But Phyllida, my Phyllida!
  She takes her buckled shoon,
When we go out a-courting
  Beneath the harvest moon.

The ladies of St. James's
  Wear satin on their backs;
They sit all night at *Ombre*,
  With candles all of wax:
But Phyllida, my Phyllida!
  She dons her russet gown,
And runs to gather May dew
  Before the world is down.

The ladies of St. James's!
  They are so fine and fair,
You'd think a box of essences
  Was broken in the air:
But Phyllida, my Phyllida!
  The breath of heath and furze,
When breezes blow at morning,
  Is not so fresh as hers.

The ladies of St. James's!
  They're painted to the eyes;

Their white it stays for ever,
   Their red it never dies:
But Phyllida, my Phyllida!
   Her colour comes and goes;
It trembles to a lily,—
   It wavers to a rose.

The ladies of St. James's!
   You scarce can understand
The half of all their speeches,
   Their phrases are so grand:
But Phyllida, my Phyllida!
   Her shy and simple words
Are clear as after rain-drops
   The music of the birds.

The ladies of St. James's
   They have their fits and freaks;
They smile on you—for seconds,
   They frown on you—for weeks;
But Phyllida, my Phyllida!
   Come either storm or shine,
From Shrove-tide unto Shrove-tide,
   Is always true—and mine.

My Phyllida! my Phyllida!
   I care not though they heap

              The hearts of all St. James's,
                And give me all to keep;
              I care not whose the beauties
                Of all the world may be,
              For Phyllida—for Phyllida
                Is all the world to me!

"GOOD NIGHT, BABETTE!"

"*Si vieillesse pouvait!—*"

SCENE.—*A small neat Room. In a high Voltaire Chair sits a white-haired old Gentleman.*

MONSIEUR VIEUXBOIS. BABETTE.

M. VIEUXBOIS (*turning querulously*)

Day of my life! Where *can* she get?
BABETTE! I say! BABETTE!—BABETTE!!

BABETTE (*entering hurriedly*)

Coming, M'sieu! If M'sieu' speaks
So loud he won't be well for weeks!

M. VIEUXBOIS

Where have you been?

BABETTE

                      Why, M'sieu' knows :—
April ! . . . Ville-d'Avray ! . . . Ma'am'selle ROSE !

M. VIEUXBOIS

Ah ! I am old,—and I forget.
Was the place growing green, BABETTE ?

BABETTE

But of a greenness !—yes, M'sieu !
And then the sky so blue !—so blue !
And when I dropped my *immortelle*,
How the birds sang !
      (*Lifting her apron to her eyes*)
                    This poor Ma'am'selle !

M. VIEUXBOIS

You're a good girl, BABETTE, but she,—
She was an Angel, verily.
Sometimes I think I see her yet
Stand smiling by the cabinet ;
And once, I know, she peeped and laughed
Betwixt the curtains . . .
                    Where's the draught ?
    (*She gives him a cup*)
Now I shall sleep, I think, BABETTE ;—
Sing me your Norman *chansonnette*.

BABETTE (*sings*)

" Once at the Angelus
(Ere I was dead),
Angels all glorious
Came to my Bed;—
Angels in blue and white
Crowned on the Head."

M. VIEUXBOIS (*drowsily*)

"She was an Angel"..."Once she laughed"...
What, was I dreaming?
                     Where's the draught?

BABETTE (*showing the empty cup*)

The draught, M'sieu?

M. VIEUXBOIS

         How I forget!
I am so old! But sing, BABETTE!

BABETTE (*sings*)

" One was the Friend I left
Stark in the Snow;
One was the Wife that died
Long,—long ago;
One was the Love I lost...
How could she know?"

    M. VIEUXBOIS (*murmuring*)
Ah, PAUL!... old PAUL!... EULALIE too!
And ROSE!... And O! "the sky so blue!"

    BABETTE (*sings*)
 "*One had my Mother's eyes,*
  Wistful and mild;
 One had my Father's face;
  One was a Child:
 All of them bent to me,—
  Bent down and smiled!"
(He is asleep!)

   M. VIEUXBOIS (*almost inaudibly*)
   How I forget!"
"I am so old!... "Good night, BABETTE!"

THE BALLAD OF THE ARMADA

King Philip had vaunted his claims;
 He had sworn for a year he would sack us;
With an army of heathenish names
 He was coming to fagot and stack us;
 Like the thieves of the sea he would track us,

And shatter our ships on the main ;
   But we had bold Neptune to back us,—
And where are the galleons of Spain ?

His carackes were christened of dames
   To the kirtles whereof he would tack us ;
With his saints and his gilded stern-frames,
   He had thought like an egg-shell to crack us ;
   Now Howard may get to his Flaccus,
And Drake to his Devon again,
   And Hawkins bowl rubbers to Bacchus,
For where are the galleons of Spain ?

Let his Majesty hang to St. James
   The axe that he whetted to hack us ;
He must play at some lustier games
   Or at sea he can hope to out-thwack us ;
   To his mines of Peru he would pack us
To tug at his bullet and chain ;
   Alas! that his Greatness should lack us !—
But where are the galleons of Spain ?

ENVOY

Gloriana !—the Don may attack us
Whenever his stomach be fain ;
   He must reach us before he can rack us, . . .
And where are the galleons of Spain ?

O

IN AFTER DAYS

In after days when grasses high
O'er-top the stone where I shall lie,
   Though ill or well the world adjust
   My slender claim to honoured dust,
I shall not question nor reply.

I shall not see the morning sky;
I shall not hear the night-wind sigh;
   I shall be mute, as all men must
      In after days!

But yet, now living, fain would I
That some one then should testify,
   Saying—" He held his pen in trust
   To Art, not serving shame or lust."
Will none?—Then let my memory die
      In after days!

AUGUSTA WEBSTER

Born 1840

IF

If I should die this night, (as well might be,
  So pain has on my weakness worked its will),
And they should come at morn and look on me

Lying more white than I am wont, and still
  In the strong silence of unchanging sleep,
And feel upon my brow the deepening chill,

And know we gathered to His time-long keep,
  The quiet watcher over all men's rest,
And weep as those around a death-bed weep—

There would no anguish throb my vacant breast,
  No tear-drop trickle down my stony cheek,
No smile of long farewell say " Calm is best."

I should not answer aught that they should speak,
  Nor look my meaning out of earnest eyes,
Nor press the reverent hands that mine should seek ;

But, lying there in such an awful guise,
  Like some strange presence from a world unknown
Unmoved by any human sympathies,

Seem strange to them, and dreadfully alone,
  Vacant to love of theirs or agony,
Having no pulse in union with their own.

Gazing henceforth upon infinity
  With a calm consciousness devoid of change,
Watching the current of the years pass by,

And watching the long cycles onward range,
  With stronger vision of their perfect whole,
As one whom time and space from them estrange.

And they might mourn and say " The parted soul
  " Is gone out of our love ; we spend in vain
" A tenderness that cannot reach its goal."

Yet I might still perchance with them remain
  In spirit, being free from laws of mould,
Still comprehending human joy and pain.

Ah me ! but if I knew them as of old,
  Clasping them in vain arms, they unaware,
And mourned to find my kisses leave them cold,

And sought still some part of their life to share
  Still standing by them, hoping they might see,
And seemed to them but as the viewless air !

For so once came it in a dream to me,
　And in my heart it seemed a pang too deep,
A shadow having human life to be.

For it at least would be long perfect sleep
　Unknowing Being and all Past to lie,
Void of the growing Future, in God's keep :

But such a knowledge would be misery
　Too great to be believed.　Yet if the dead
In a diviner mood might still be nigh,

Their former life unto their death so wed
　That they could watch their loved with heavenly eye,
That were a thing to joy in, not to dread.

HARRIET E. HAMILTON KING
Born 1840

From "THE DISCIPLES"

And now I speak, not with the bird's free voice,
Who wakens the first mornings of the year
With low sweet pipings, dropped among the dew;
Then stops and ceases, saying, "All the spring
And summer lies before me; I will sleep;
And sing a little louder, while the green
Builds up the scattered spaces of the boughs;
And faster, while the grasses grow to flower
Beneath my music; let the full song grow
With the full year, till the heart too is filled."

But as the Swan (who has pass'd through the spring,
And found it snow still in the white North land,
And over perilous wilds of Northern seas,
White wings above the white and wintry waves,
Has won, through night and battle of the blasts,
Breathless, alone, without one note or cry)

Sinks into summer by a land at last;
And knows his wings are broken, and the floods
Will bear him with them whither God shall will;—
And knows he has one hour between the tides;
And sees the salt and silent marshes spread
Before him outward to the shining sea,
Whereon was never any music heard.—

I am not proud for anything of mine,
Done, dreamed, or suffered, but for this alone:
That the great orb of that great human soul
Did once deflect and draw this orb of mine,
(In the shadow of it, not the sunward side),
Until it touched and trembled on the line
By which my orbit crossed the plane of his;
And heard the music of that glorious sphere
Resound a moment; and so passed again,
Vibrating with it, out on its own way;
Where, intertwined with others, it may yet
Spin through its manifold mazes of ellipse,
Amid the clangour of a myriad more,
Revolving, and the dimness of the depths
Remotest, through the shadows without shape,
Arcs of aphelion, silences of snow:
But henceforth doth no more go spiritless,
But knows its own pole through the whirling ways,
And hath beheld the Angel of the Sun,

And yearns to it, and follows thereunto;
And feels the conscious thrill that doth transmute
Inertia to obedience, underneath
The ordered sway of balanced counter-force,
That speedeth all life onward through all space;
And hears the key-note of all various worlds,
Caught and combined in one vast harmony,
And floated down the perfect Heavens of God.

From "AGESILAO MILANO"

Sunrise! and it is summer, and the morning
    Waits glorified
An hour hence, when the cool clear rose-cloud gathers
    About heaven's eastern side,
And down the azure grottoes where the bathers
    Loose the tired limbs, a lovely light will glide.

Fold after fold the winding waves of opal
    The sands will drown;
And when the morning-star amid the pearly
    Light of the east goes down,
Then my star shall arise, and late and early
    Shine for a jewel in the Master's crown.

Mazzini, Master, singer of the sunrise!
  Knowest thou me?
I held thy hand once, and the summer lightning
  Still of thy smile I see;
Me thou rememberest not amidst the heightening
  Vision of God, and of God's Will to be.

But thou wilt hear of me, by noon to-morrow,
  And henceforth I
Shall be to thee a memory and a token
  Out of the starry sky;
And when my soul unto thy soul hath spoken,
  Enough,—I shall not wholly pass nor die.

Italia, when thou comest to thy kingdom,
  Remember me!
Me, who on this thy night of shame and sorrow
  Was scourged and slain with thee;
Me, who upon thy resurrection morrow
  Shall stand among thy sons beside thy knee.

Shalt thou not be one day, indeed, O Mother,
  Enthroned of all,
To the world's vision as to ours now only,
  At Rome for festival;
Around thee gathered all thy lost and lonely
  And loyal ones, that failed not at thy call.

With golden lyre, or violet robe of mourning,
    Or battle-scar;—
And one shall stand more glorious than the others,
    He of the Morning-Star,
Whose face lights all the faces of his brothers,
    Out of the silvery northern land afar.

But grant to me there, unto all beholders,
    Bare to the skies,
To stand with bleeding hands, and feet, and shoulders,
    And rapt, unflinching eyes,
And locked lips, yielding to the question-holders
    Nor moanings, nor beseechings, nor replies.

Is the hour hard? Too soon it will be over,
    Too sweet, too sore;
The arms of Death fold over me with rapture,
    Life knew not heretofore;
Heaven will be peace, but I shall not recapture,
    The passion of this hour, for evermore.

ROBERT WILLIAMS BUCHANAN
Born 1841

FROM "WHITE ROSE AND RED"

DROWSIETOWN

O so drowsy! In a daze
Sweating 'mid the golden haze,
With its smithy like an eye
Glaring bloodshot at the sky,
And its one white row of street
Carpetted so green and sweet,
And the loungers smoking still
Over gate and window-sill;
Nothing coming, nothing going,
Locusts grating, one cock crowing,
Few things moving up or down,
All things drowsy—Drowsietown!

Thro' the fields with sleepy gleam,
Drowsy, drowsy steals the stream,

Touching with its azure arms
Upland fields and peaceful farms,
Gliding with a twilight tide
Where the dark elms shade its side;
Twining, pausing sweet and bright
Where the lilies sail so white;
Winding in its sedgy hair
Meadow-sweet and iris fair;
Humming as it hies along
Monotones of sleepy song;
Deep and dimpled, bright nut-brown,
Flowing into Drowsietown.

Far as eye can see, around,
Upland fields and farms are found,
Floating prosperous and fair
In the mellow misty air:
Apple-orchards, blossoms blowing
Up above,—and clover growing
Red and scented round the knees
Of the old moss-silvered trees.
Hark! with drowsy deep refrain,
In the distance rolls a wain;
As its dull sound strikes the ear,
Other kindred sounds grow clear—
Drowsy all—the soft breeze blowing,
Locusts grating, one cock crowing,

Cries like voices in a dream
Far away amid the gleam,
Then the waggons rumbling down
Thro' the lanes to Drowsietown.

Drowsy? Yea!—but idle? Nay!
Slowly, surely, night and day,
Humming low, well greased with oil,
Turns the wheel of human toil.
Here no grating gruesome cry
Of spasmodic industry;
No rude clamour, mad and mean,
Of a horrible machine!
Strong yet peaceful, surely roll'd,
Winds the wheel that whirls the gold.
Year by year the rich rare land
Yields its store to human hand—
Year by year the stream makes fat
Every field and meadow-flat—
Year by year the orchards fair
Gather glory from the air,
Redden, ripen, freshly fed,
Their bright balls of golden red.
Thus, most prosperous and strong,
Flows the stream of life along
Six slow days! wains come and go,
Wheat-fields ripen, squashes grow,

Cattle browse on hill and dale,
Milk foams sweetly in the pail,
Six days: on the seventh day,
Toil's low murmur dies away—
All is husht save drowsy din
Of the waggons rolling in,
Drawn amid the plenteous meads
By small fat and sleepy steeds.
Folks with faces fresh as fruit
Sit therein or trudge afoot,
Brightly drest for all to see,
In their seventh-day finery:
Farmers in their breeches tight,
Snowy cuffs, and buckles bright;
Ancient dames and matrons staid
In their silk and flower'd brocade,
Prim and tall, with soft brows knitted,
Silken aprons, and hands mitted;
Haggard women, dark of face,
Of the old lost Indian race;
Maidens happy-eyed and fair,
With bright ribbons in their hair,
Trip along, with eyes cast down,
Thro' the streets of Drowsietown.

Drowsy in the summer day
In the meeting-house sit they:

'Mid the high-back'd pews they doze,
Like bright garden-flowers in rows;
And old Parson Pendon, big
In his gown and silver'd wig,
Drones above in periods fine
Sermons like old flavour'd wine—
Crusted well with keeping long
In the darkness, and not strong.
O! so drowsily he drones
In his rich and sleepy tones,
While the great door, swinging wide,
Shows the bright green street outside,
And the shadows as they pass
On the golden sunlit grass.
Then the mellow organ blows,
And the sleepy music flows,
And the folks their voices raise
In old unctuous hymns of praise,
Fit to reach some ancient god
Half asleep with drowsy nod.
Deep and lazy, clear and low,
Doth the oily organ grow!
Then with sudden golden cease
Comes a silence and a peace
Then a murmur, all alive,
As of bees within a hive;
And they swarm with quiet feet

Out into the sunny street:
There, at hitching-post and gate
Do the steeds and waggons wait.
Drawn in groups, the gossips talk,
Shaking hands before they walk;
Maids and lovers steal away,
Smiling hand in hand, to stray
By the river, and to say
Drowsy love in the old way—
Till the sleepy sun shines down
On the roofs of Drowsietown.

In the great marsh, far beyond
Street and building, lies the Pond,
Gleaming like a silver shield
In the midst of wood and field;
There on sombre days you see
Anglers old in reverie,
Fishing feebly morn to night
For the pickerel so bright.
From the woods of beech and fir,
Dull blows of the woodcutter
Faintly sound; and haply, too,
Comes the cat-owl's wild "tuhoo"!
Drown'd by distance, dull and deep,
Like a dark sound heard in sleep;—

And a cock may answer, down
In the depths of Drowsietown.

Such is Drowsietown—but nay!
Was, not *is*, my song should say—
Such *was* summer long ago
In this town so sleepy and slow.
Change has come: thro' wood and dale
Runs the demon of the rail,
And the Drowsietown of yore
Is not drowsy any more!

WILLIAM JOHN COURTHOPE.

Born 1842

From "THE PARADISE OF BIRDS"

CHORUS OF HUMAN SOULS

Mortals who attempt the seas
Where man's breath and blood must freeze—
You whom Fortune, by despite,
Destiny, or daring, carry
Farther in the four months' night
Than M'Clintock, Sabine, Parry,
Hayes, or Kane—
Say, we charge ye, why ye come
Where humanity is dumb;
Is it but to reive and harry,
Or for gain,
That you break the arctic barriers where
    feathered spirits reign?

Are you whalers, blown astray
In the chase through Baffin's Bay?

Or men tired of the sun,
Human thought and speech and feature,
That you seek, what all things shun,
Night, that hides each kind and creature?
Have hard times
Driven you up, in hopes of food,
To this landless latitude?
Know ye not, indeed, that Nature
In these climes
For our race produces nothing but requital for
    our crimes?

Back, we do beseech ye, back
To the ice-floe and the pack!
If your hand has driven a quill,
Clipped a wing, or plucked a feather,
Were your purpose good or ill,
Ye are ruined altogether,
Body and soul!
We were men who speak these words,
But for harm we did the birds
Now are beaten in this weather,
Past control,
Round the Paradise that holds the Aviary of the
    Pole.

For our crimes are here decreed
Pains proportioned to each deed:

As on earth we played our parts,
Such in Purgatory our measure:
But behold our human hearts
Are transfigured, and old pleasure
Here is pain:
Some become the birds they slew;
Some fruitlessly pursue
Feathered phantoms; all at leisure,
In one strain,
Swear the birds should live for ever could *they*
    live their lives again.

Therefore, back! and if one bird
By your dwelling still be heard
(Since for all this winter none
Pass our barriers), we implore ye
Leave this singer in the sun,
Telling the live world our story;
For 'tis meet
That the infidel should so
By report believe the woe,
Waiting all in Purgatory,
Who entreat
Cruelly with death or dungeon things so simple
    and so sweet.

CHORUS OF BIRDS

We wish to declare how the Birds of the air all high
  Institutions designed,
And holding in awe, art, science, and law, delivered
  the same to mankind.
To begin with: of old Man went naked and cold
  whenever it pelted or froze,
Till we showed him how feathers were proof against
  weathers; with that he bethought him of hose.
And next it was plain that he in the rain was forced
  to sit dripping and blind,
While the reed-warbler swung in a nest with her young,
  deep-sheltered and warm from the wind.
So our homes in the boughs made him think of the
  house; and the swallow, to help him invent,
Revealed the best way to economise clay, and bricks
  to combine with cement.
The knowledge withal of the carpenter's awl is drawn
  from the nuthatch's bill,
And the sand-marten's pains in the hazel-clad lanes
  instructed the mason to drill.
Is there one of the arts more dear to men's hearts, to
  the birds' inspiration they owe it,
For the nightingale first sweet music rehearsed, prima
  donna, composer, and poet.

The owl's dark retreats showed sages the sweets of
    brooding to spin or unravel
Fine webs in one's brain, philosophical, vain,—the
    swallows the pleasures of travel,
Who chirped in such strain of Greece, Italy, Spain,
    and Egypt, that men, when they heard,
Were mad to fly forth from their nests in the north,
    and follow the tail of the bird.
Besides, it is true to our wisdom is due the knowledge
    of sciences all,
And chiefly those rare Metaphysics of air men Me-
    teorology call.
For, indeed, it is said a kingfisher when dead has his
    science alive in him still;
And, hung up, he will show how the wind means to
    blow, and turn to the point with his bill.
And men in their words acknowledge the birds' erudi-
    tion in weather and star;
For they say, " 'Twill be dry—the swallow is high;"
    or, " Rain—for the chough is afar."
'Twas the rooks who taught men vast pamphlets to
    pen upon Social Compact and Law,
And Parliaments hold, as themselves did of old, ex-
    claiming " Hear, hear," for " Caw, caw!"
When they build, if one steal, so great is their zeal for
    justice, that all, at a pinch,
Without legal test will demolish his nest, and hence is
    the trial by Lynch.

And whence arose love? Go ask of the dove, or behold how the titmouse, unresting,
Still early and late ever sings by his mate, to lighten her labours of nesting.
Their bonds never gall, though the leaves shoot and fall, and the seasons roll round in their course,
For their Marriage each year grows more lovely and dear, and they know not decrees of Divorce.
That these things are Truth we have learned from our youth, for our hearts to our customs incline,
As the rivers that roll from the fount of our soul, immortal, unchanging, divine.
Man, simple and old, in his ages of gold, derived from our teaching true light,
And deemed it his praise in his ancestors' ways to govern his footsteps aright.
But the fountain of woes, Philosophy, rose, and what betwixt Reason and Whim,
He has splintered our rules into sections and schools, so the world is made bitter for him.
But the birds, since on earth they discovered the worth of their souls, and resolved, with a vow,
No custom to change for a new or a strange have attained unto Paradise now.

FREDERIC W. H. MYERS
Born 1843

From "ST. PAUL"

See, where a fireship in mid ocean blazes
    Lone on the battlements a swimmer stands,
Looks for a help, and findeth not, and raises
    High for a moment melancholy hands;

Then the sad ship, to her own funeral flaring,
    Holds him no longer in her arms, for he
Simple and strong, and desolate, and daring,
    Leaps to the great embraces of the sea.

So when around me for my soul's affrighting,
    Madly red-litten of the woe within,
Faces of men and deeds of their delighting
    Stare in a lurid cruelty of sin,

Thus, as I weary me, and long, and languish,
    Nowise availing from that pain to part,—
Desperate tides of the whole great world's anguish
    Forced thro' the channels of a single heart,—

Then let me feel how infinite around me
    Floats the eternal peace that is to be,
Rush from the demons, for my King has found me,
    Leap from the universe and plunge in Thee!

TENERIFFE

Atlantid islands, phantom-fair,
    Throned on the solitary seas,
Immersed in amethystine air,
    Haunt of Hesperides!
Farewell! I leave Madeira thus
Drowned in a sunset glorious,
The Holy Harbour fading far
Beneath a blaze of cinnabar.

What sights had burning eve to show
    From Tacoronte's orange bowers,
From palmy headlands of Ycod,
    From Orotava's flowers!
When Palma or Canary lay
Cloud-cinctured in the crimson day—
Sea, and sea-wrack, and rising higher
Those purple peaks 'twixt cloud and fire.

But oh the cone aloft and clear
    Where Atlas in the heavens withdrawn
To hemisphere and hemisphere
    Disparts the dark and dawn!
O vaporous waves that roll and press!
Fire-opalescent wilderness!
O pathway by the sunbeams ploughed
Betwixt those pouring walls of cloud!

We watched adown that glade of fire
    Celestrial Iris floating free,
We saw the cloudlets keep in choir
    Their dances on the sea;
The scarlet, huge, and quivering sun
Feared his due hour was overrun,—
On us the last he blazed, and hurled
His glory on Columbus' world.

Then ere our eyes the change could tell,
    Or feet bewildered turn again,
From Teneriffe the darkness fell
    Head-foremost on the main:—
A hundred leagues was seaward flown
The gloom of Teyde's towering cone,—
Full half the height of heaven's blue
That monstrous shadow overflew.

Then all is twilight; pile on pile
    The scattered flocks of cloudland close,
An alabaster wall, erewhile
    Much redder than the rose!—
Falls like a sleep on souls forspent
Majestic Night's abandonment;
Wakes like a waking life afar
Hung o'er the sea one eastern star.

O Nature's glory, Nature's youth!
    Perfected sempiternal whole!
And is the World's in very truth
    An impercipient soul?
Or doth that Spirit, past our ken,
Live a profounder life than men,
Awaits our passing days, and thus
In secret places calls to us?

O fear not thou, whate'er befall
    Thy transient individual breath,—
Behold, thou knowest not at all
    What kind of thing is Death;
And here indeed might Death be fair,
If Death be dying into air,—
If souls evanished mix with thee,
Illumined heaven, eternal sea.

SIMMENTHAL

Far off the old snows ever new
With silver edges cleft the blue
    Aloft, alone, divine;
The sunny meadows silent slept,
Silence the sombre armies kept,
    The vanguard of the pine.

In that thin air the birds are still,
No ringdove murmurs on the hill
    Nor mating cushat calls;
But gay cicalas singing sprang,
And waters from the forest sang
    The song of waterfalls.

O Fate! a few enchanted hours
Beneath the firs, among the flowers,
    High on the lawn we lay,
Then turned again, contented well,
While bright about us flamed and fell
    The rapture of the day.

And softly with a guileless awe
Beyond the purple lake she saw
    The embattled summits glow;

    She saw the glories melt in one,
The round moon rise, while yet the sun
       Was rosy on the snow.

Then like a newly-singing bird
The child's soul in her bosom stirred;
       I know not what she sung:—
Because the soft wind caught her hair,
Because the golden moon was fair,
       Because her heart was young.

I would her sweet soul ever may
Look thus from those glad eyes and grey,
       Unfearing, undefiled:
I love her; when her face I see,
Her simple presence wakes in me
       The imperishable child.

ROBERT BRIDGES

Born 1844

ELEGY

ON A LADY, WHOM GRIEF FOR THE DEATH OF HER BETROTHED KILLED.

Assemble, all ye maidens, at the door,
   And all ye loves assemble; far and wide
Proclaim the bridal, that proclaimed before
   Has been deferred to this late eventide:
     For on this night the bride,
     The days of her betrothal over,
Leaves the parental hearth for evermore;
To-night the bride goes forth to meet her lover.

Reach down the wedding vesture, that has lain
   Yet all unvisited, the silken gown:
Bring out the bracelets, and the golden chain
   Her dearer friends provided: sere and brown
     Bring out the festal crown,
     And set it on her forehead lightly:

Though it be withered, twine no wreath again;
This only is the crown she can wear rightly.

Cloke her in ermine, for the night is cold,
    And wrap her warmly, for the night is long,
In pious hands the flaming torches hold,
    While her attendants, chosen from among
        Her faithful virgin throng,
      May lay her in her cedar litter;
Decking her coverlet with sprigs of gold,
Roses, and lilies white that best befit her.

Sound flutes and tabors, that the bridal be
    Not without music, nor with these alone;
But let the viol lead the melody,
    With lesser intervals, and plaintive moan
        Of sinking semitone;
      And, all in choir, the virgin voices
Rest not from singing in skilled harmony
The song that aye the bridegroom's ear rejoices,

Let the priests go before, arrayed in white,
    And let the dark stoled minstrels follow slow,
Next they that bear her, honoured on this night,
    And then the maidens, in a double row,
        Each singing soft and low,
      And each on high a torch upstaying:

Unto her lover lead her forth with light,
With music, and with singing, and with praying.

'Twas at this sheltering hour he nightly came,
    And found her trusty window open wide,
And knew the signal of the timorous flame,
    That long the restless curtain would not hide
        Her form that stood beside;
    As scarce she dared to be delighted,
Listening to that sweet tale, that is no shame
To faithful lovers, that their hearts have plighted.

But now for many days the dewy grass
    Has shown no markings of his feet at morn:
And watching she has seen no shadow pass
    The moonlit walk, and heard no music borne
        Upon her ear forlorn.
    In vain has she looked out to greet him;
He has not come, he will not come, alas!
So let us bear her out where she must meet him.

Now to the river bank the priests are come:
    The bark is ready to receive its freight:
Let some prepare her place therein, and some
    Embark the litter with its slender weight:
        The rest stand by in state,
    And sing her a safe passage over;

While she is oared across to her new home,
Into the arms of her expectant lover.

And thou, O lover, that art on the watch,
  Where, on the banks of the forgetful streams,
The pale indifferent ghosts wander, and snatch
    The sweeter moments of their broken dreams,—
      Thou, when the torchlight gleams,
  When thou shalt see the slow procession,
And when thine ears the fitful music catch,
Rejoice! for thou art near to thy possession.

MY SONG

I have loved flowers that fade,
  Within whose magic tents
Rich hues have marriage made
  With sweet unmemoried scents:
A joy of love at sight,—
A honeymoon delight,
That ages in an hour:—
My song be like a flower!

I have loved airs, that die
  Before their charm is writ

Upon the liquid sky
   Trembling to welcome it.
Notes, that with pulse of fire
Proclaim the spirit's desire,
Then die, and are nowhere :—
My song be like an air!

Die, song, die like a breath,
   And wither as a bloom:
Fear not a flowery death,
   Dread not an airy tomb!
Fly with delight, fly hence!
'Twas thine love's tender sense
To feast, and on thy bier
Beauty shall shed a tear.

ANDREW LANG

Born 1844

BALLADE OF SLEEP

The hours are passing slow,
I hear their weary tread
Clang from the tower, and go
Back to their kinsfolk dead.
Sleep! death's twin brother dread!
Why dost thou scorn me so?
The wind's voice overhead
Long wakeful here I know,
And music from the steep
Where waters fall and flow.
Wilt thou not hear me, Sleep?

All sounds that might bestow
Rest on the fever'd bed,
All slumb'rous sounds and low
Are mingled here and wed,
And bring no drowsihead.

Shy dreams flit to and fro
With shadowy hair dispread;
With wistful eyes that glow,
And silent robes that sweep.
Thou wilt not hear me; no?
Wilt thou not hear me, Sleep?

What cause hast thou to show
Of sacrifice unsped?
Of all thy slaves below
I most have labourèd
With service sung and said;
Have cull'd such buds as blow,
Soft poppies white and red,
Where thy still gardens grow,
And Lethe's waters weep.
Why, then, art thou my foe?
Wilt thou not hear me, Sleep?

ENVOY

Prince, ere the dark be shred
By golden shafts, ere low
And long the shadows creep:
Lord of the wand of lead,
Soft-footed as the snow,
Wilt thou not hear me, Sleep!

BALLADE OF HIS CHOICE OF A SEPULCHRE

Here I'd come when weariest!
    Here the breast
Of the Windburg's tufted over
Deep with bracken; here his crest
    Takes the west,
Where the wide-winged hawk doth hover.

Silent here are lark and plover;
    In the cover
Deep below the cushat best
Loves his mate, and croons above her
    O'er their nest,
Where the wide-winged hawk doth hover.

Bring me here, Life's tired-out guest,
    To the blest
Bed that waits the weary rover,
Here should failure be confessed;
    Ends my quest,
Where the wide-winged hawk doth hover!

ENVOY

Friend, or stranger kind, or lover,
Ah, fulfil a last behest,
   Let me rest
Where the wide-winged hawk doth hover!

NATURAL THEOLOGY

*ἐπεὶ ἐπὶ τοῦτον ὄιομαι ἀθανάτοισιν
εὔχεσθαι· Πάντες δὲ θεῶν χατέουσ' ἄνθρωποι.*
                       Od. iii. 47.

"Once CAGN was like a father, kind and good,
   But He was spoiled by fighting many things;
He wars upon the lions in the wood,
   And breaks the Thunder-bird's tremendous wings;
But still we cry to Him,—*We are thy brood—
   O Cagn, be merciful!* and us He brings
To herds of elands, and great store of food,
   And in the desert opens water-springs."

So Qing, King Nqsha's Bushman hunter, spoke
   Beside the camp-fire, by the fountain fair,
When all were weary, and soft clouds of smoke
   Were fading, fragrant, in the twilit air:
And suddenly in each man's heart there woke
   A pang, a sacred memory of prayer.

EDMUND GOSSE

Born 1849

LYING IN THE GRASS

Between two golden tufts of summer grass,
I see the world through hot air as through glass,
And by my face sweet lights and colours pass.

Before me, dark against the fading sky,
I watch three mowers mowing, as I lie:
With brawny arms they sweep in harmony.

Brown English faces by the sun burnt red,
Rich glowing colour on bare throat and head,
My heart would leap to watch them, were I dead!

And in my strong young living as I lie,
I seem to move with them in harmony,—
A fourth is mowing, and that fourth am I.

The music of the scythes that glide and leap,
The young men whistling as their great arms sweep,
And all the perfume and sweet sense of sleep,

The weary butterflies that droop their wings,
The dreamy nightingale that hardly sings,
And all the lassitude of happy things,

Is mingling with the warm and pulsing blood
That gushes through my veins a languid flood,
And feeds my spirit as the sap a bud.

Behind the mowers, on the amber air,
A dark-green beech wood rises, still and fair,
A white path winding up it like a stair.

And see that girl, with pitcher on her head,
And clean white apron on her gown of red,—
Her even-song of love is but half-said:

She waits the youngest mower. Now he goes;
Her cheeks are redder than the wild blush-rose:
They climb up where the deepest shadows close.

But though they pass, and vanish, I am there.
I watch his rough hands meet beneath her hair,
Their broken speech sounds sweet to me like prayer.

Ah! now the rosy children come to play,
And romp and struggle with the new-mown hay;
Their clear high voices sound from far away.

They know so little why the world is sad,
They dig themselves warm graves and yet are glad;
Their muffled screams and laughter make me mad!

I long to go and play among them there;
Unseen, like wind, to take them by the hair,
And gently make their rosy cheeks more fair.

The happy children! full of frank surprise,
And sudden whims and innocent ecstasies;
What godhead sparkles from their liquid eyes!

No wonder round those urns of mingled clays
That Tuscan potters fashioned in old days,
And coloured like the torrid earth ablaze,

We find the little gods and loves portrayed,
Through ancient forests wandering undismayed,
And fluting hymns of pleasure unafraid.

They knew, as I do now, what keen delight,
A strong man feels to watch the tender flight
Of little children playing in his sight;

What pure sweet pleasure, and what sacred love,
Comes drifting down upon us from above,
In watching how their limbs and features move.

I do not hunger for a well-stored mind,
I only wish to live my life, and find
My heart in unison with all mankind.

My life is like the single dewy star
That trembles on the horizon's primrose-bar,—
A microcosm where all things living are.

And if, among the noiseless grasses, Death
Should come behind and take away my breath,
I should not rise as one who sorroweth;

For I should pass, but all the world would be
Full of desire and young delight and glee,
And why should men be sad through loss of me?

The light is flying; in the silver-blue
The young moon shines from her bright window
    through:
The mowers are all gone, and I go too.

THE RETURN OF THE SWALLOWS

"Out in the meadows the young grass springs,
    Shivering with sap," said the larks, "and we
Shoot into air with our strong young wings,
    Spirally up over level and lea;

Come, O Swallows, and fly with us
Now that horizons are luminous!
  Evening and morning the world of light,
  Spreading and kindling, is infinite!"

Far away, by the sea in the south,
  The hills of olive and slopes of fern
Whiten and glow in the sun's long drouth,
  Under the heavens that beam and burn;
And all the swallows were gathered there
Flitting about in the fragrant air,
  And heard no sound from the larks, but flew
  Flashing under the blinding blue.

Out of the depths of their soft rich throats
  Languidly fluted the thrushes, and said:
"Musical thought in the mild air floats,
  Spring is coming and winter is dead!
Come, O Swallows, and stir the air,
For the buds are all bursting unaware,
  And the drooping eaves and the elm-trees long
  To hear the sound of your low sweet song."

Over the roofs of the white Algiers,
  Flashingly shadowing the bright bazaar,
Flitted the swallows, and not one hears
  The call of the thrushes from far, from far;

Sighed the thrushes; then, all at once,
Broke out singing the old sweet tones,
   Singing the bridal of sap and shoot,
   The tree's slow life between root and fruit.

But just when the dingles of April flowers
   Shine with the earliest daffodils,
When, before sunrise, the cold clear hours
   Gleam with a promise that noon fulfils,—
Deep in the leafage the cuckoo cried,
Perched on a spray by a rivulet-side,
   Swallows, O Swallows, come back again
   To swoop and herald the April rain.

And something awoke in the slumbering heart
   Of the alien birds in their African air,
And they paused, and alighted, and twittered apart,
   And met in the broad white dreamy square,
And the sad slave woman, who lifted up
From the fountain her broad-lipped earthen cup,
   Said to herself, with a weary sigh,
   "To-morrow the swallows will northward fly!"

THE CHARCOAL-BURNER

He lives within the hollow wood,
   From one clear dell he seldom ranges;
His daily toil in solitude
   Revolves, but never changes.

A still old man, with grizzled beard,
   Grey eye, bent shape, and smoke-tanned features,
His quiet footstep is not feared
   By shyest woodland creatures.

I love to watch the pale blue spire
   His scented labour builds above it;
I track the woodland by his fire,
   And, seen afar, I love it.

It seems among the serious trees
   The emblem of a living pleasure,
It animates the silences
   As with a tuneful measure.

And dream not that such humdrum ways
   Fold naught of nature's charm around him;

The mystery of soundless days
   Hath sought for him and found him.

He hides within his simple brain
   An instinct innocent and holy,
The music of a wood-bird's strain,—
   Not blithe, nor melancholy,

But hung upon the calm content
   Of wholesome leaf and bough and blossom—
An unecstatic ravishment
   Born in a rustic bosom.

He knows the moods of forest things,
   He feels, in his own speechless fashion,
For helpless forms of fur and wings
   A mild paternal passion.

Within his horny hand he holds
   The warm brood of the ruddy squirrel;
Their bushy mother storms and scolds,
   But knows no sense of peril.

The dormouse shares his crumb of cheese,
   His homeward trudge the rabbits follow;
He finds, in angles of the trees,
   The cup-nest of the swallow.

And through this sympathy, perchance,
  The beating heart of life he reaches
Far more than we who idly dance
  An hour beneath the beeches.

Our science and our empty pride,
  Our busy dream of introspection,
To God seem vain and poor beside
  This dumb, sincere reflection.

Yet he will die unsought, unknown,
  A nameless head-stone stand above him,
And the vast woodland, vague and lone,
  Be all that's left to love him.

TWO POINTS OF VIEW

    If I forget,—
May joy pledge this weak heart to sorrow!
    If I forget,—
May my soul's coloured summer borrow
The hueless tones of storm and rain,
Of ruth and terror, shame and pain,—
    If I forget!

        Though you forget,—
There is no binding code for beauty;
        Though you forget,—
Love was your charm, but not your duty;
And life's worst breeze must never bring
A ruffle to your silken wing,
        Though you forget.

        If I forget,—
The salt creek may forget the ocean;
        If I forget,—
The heart whence flows my heart's bright motion,
May I sink meanlier than the worst,
Abandoned, outcast, crushed, accurst,—
        If I forget!

        Though you forget,—
No word of mine shall mar your pleasure;
        Though you forget,—
You filled my barren life with treasure,
You may withdraw the gift you gave,
You still are lord, I still am slave,—
        Though you forget.

WALTER HERRIES POLLOCK

Born 1850

A CONQUEST

I found him openly wearing her token;
I knew that her troth could never be broken;
I laid my hand on the hilt of my sword,
He did the same and spoke not a word;
I bad him confess his villany,
He smiled, and said, 'She gave it me.'
We searched for seconds, they soon were found,
They measured our swords and measured the ground,
To save us they would not have uttered a breath,
They were ready enough to help us to death.
We fought in the midst of a wintry wood,
Till the fair white snow was red with his blood:
But his was the victory, for, as he died,
He swore by the rood that he had not lied.

ROBERT LOUIS STEVENSON

Born 1850

THE HOUSE BEAUTIFUL

A naked house, a naked moor,
A shivering pool before the door,
A garden bare of flowers and fruit
And poplars at the garden-foot;
Such is the place that I live in,
Bleak without and bare within.

Yet shall your ragged moor receive
The incomparable pomp of eve,
And the cold glories of the dawn
Behind your shivering trees be drawn ;
And when the wind from place to place
Doth the unmoored cloud-galleons chase,
Your garden gloom and gleam again,
With leaping sun, with glancing rain.
Here shall the wizard moon ascend
The heavens, in the crimson end
Of day's declining splendour ; here

The army of the stars appear.
The neighbour hollows dry and wet,
Spring shall with tender flowers beset;
And oft the morning muser see
Larks rising from the broomy lea,
And every fairy wheel and thread
Of cobweb dew-bediamonded.

When daises go, shall winter time
Silver the simple grass with rime;
Autumnal frosts enchant the pool
And make the cart-ruts beautiful;
And when snow-bright the moor expands,
How shall your children clap their hands!
To make this earth, our hermitage,
A cheerful and a changeful page,
God's bright and intricate device
Of days and seasons doth suffice.

THE CELESTIAL SURGEON

If I have faltered more or less
In my great task of happiness;
If I have moved among my race
And shown no glorious morning face;

If beams from happy human eyes
Have moved me not; if morning skies,
Books, and my food, and summer rain
Knocked on my sullen heart in vain;—
Lord, thy most pointed pleasure take
And stab my spirit broad awake;
Or, Lord, if too obdurate I,
Choose Thou, before that spirit die,
A piercing pain, a killing sin,
And to my dead heart run them in.

THE WIND

I saw you toss the kites on high
And blow the birds about the sky;
And all around I heard you pass,
Like ladies' skirts across the grass—
    O wind, a-blowing all day long,
    O wind, that sings so loud a song!

I saw the different things you did,
But always you yourself you hid.
I felt you push, I heard you call,
I could not see yourself at all—
    O wind, a-blowing all day long,
    O wind, that sings so loud a song!

O you that are so strong and cold,
O blower, are you young or old?
Are you a beast of field and tree,
Or just a stronger child than me?
  O wind, a-blowing all day long,
  O wind, that sings so loud a song!

"SAY NOT OF ME"

Say not of me that weakly I declined
The labours of my sires, and fled the sea,
The towers we founded and the lamps we lit,
To play at home with paper like a child.
But rather say: *In the afternoon of time*
A strenuous family dusted from its hands
The sand of granite, and beholding far
Along the sounding coast its pyramids
And tall memorials catch the dying sun,
Smiled well content, and to this childish task
Around the fire addressed its evening hours.

"SING CLEARLIER, MUSE"

Sing clearlier, Muse, or evermore be still,
Sing truer or no longer sing!
No more the voice of melancholy Jacques
To make a weeping echo in the hill;
But as the boy, the pirate of the spring,
From the green elm a living linnet takes,
One natural verse recapture—then be still.

THEOPHILE MARZIALS

Born 1850

SONG

There's one great bunch of stars in heaven
    That shines so sturdily,
Where good Saint Peter's sinewy hand
    Holds up the dull gold-wroughten key.

There's eke a little twinkling gem
    As green as beryl-blue can be,
The lowest bead the Blessed Virgin
    Shakes a-telling her rosary.

There's one that flashes flames and fire,
    No doubt the mighty rubicel,
That sparkles from the centre point
    I' the buckler of stout Raphael.

And also there's a little star
    So white a virgin's it must be ;—
Perhaps the lamp my love in heaven
    Hangs out to light the way for me.

A PASTORAL

Flower of the medlar,
  Crimson of the Quince,
I saw her at the blossom-time,
  And loved her ever since!
She swept the draughty pleasance,
  The blooms had left the trees,
The whilst the birds sang canticles,
  In cheery symphonies.

Whiteness of the white rose,
  Redness of the red,
She went to cut the blush-rose-buds
  To tie at the altar-head;
And some she laid in her bosom,
  And some around her brows,
And as she past, the lily-heads
  All beck'd and made their bows.

Scarlet of the poppy,
  Yellow of the corn,
The men were at the garnering,
  A-shouting in the morn;
I chased her to a pippin-tree,—
  The waking birds all whist,—

And oh! it was the sweetest kiss
   That I have ever kiss'd.

Marjorie, mint, and violets
   A-drying round us set,
'Twas all done in the faïence-room
   A-spicing marmalet;
On one tile was a satyr,
   On one a nymph at bay,
Methinks the birds will scarce be home
   To wake our wedding-day!

SONG

I dream'd I was in Sicily,
   All sky and hills and flowers;
We sat us under a citron-tree
   And courted, hours and hours.

I woke by the dunes of a bleak north-land,
   Along a lonely grave in the snow;
The salt wind rattled the ivy-band
   I'd tied at the headstone long ago.

MARGARET L. WOODS
Born 1855

TO THE FORGOTTEN DEAD

                To the forgotten dead,
Come, let us drink in silence ere we part.
To every fervent yet resolvèd heart
That brought its tameless passion and its tears,
Renunciation and laborious years,
To lay the deep foundations of our race,
To rear its stately fabric overhead
And light its pinnacles with golden grace—
                To the unhonoured dead.

                To the forgotten dead,
Whose dauntless hands were stretched to grasp the rein
Of Fate and hurl into the void again
Her thunder-hoofèd horses, rushing blind
Eastward along the courses of the wind.
Among the stars, along the wind in vain
Their souls were scattered and their blood was shed,
And nothing, nothing of them doth remain—
                To the thrice-perished dead.

MARY DARMESTETER

Born 1857

TO A DRAGON-FLY

You hail from Dream-land, Dragon-fly?
A stranger hither? So am I,
And (sooth to say) I wonder why
    We either of us came,
Are you (that shine so bright i' the air)
King Oberon's state-messenger?
Come tell me how my old friends fare,
    Is Dream-land still the same?

Who won the latest tourney fight,
King Arthur, or the Red-Cross Knight,
Or he who bore away the bright
    Renown'd Mambrino's Casque?
Is Caliban King's councillor yet?
Cross Mentor jester still and pet?
Is Suckling out of love and debt?
    Has Spenser done his task?

Say, have they settled over there,
Which is the loveliest Guinevere,
Or Gloriana, or the fair
    Young Queen of Oberon's Court?
And does Titania torment still
Mike Drayton and sweet-throated Will?
In sooth of her amours 'twas ill
    To make such merry sport.

Ah, I have been too long away!
No doubt I shall return some day,
But now I'm lost in love and may
    Not leave my lady's sight.
Mine is, (of course), the happier lot
Yet—tell them I forget them not,
My pretty gay compatriot,
    When you go home to-night.

LE ROI EST MORT

And shall I weep that Love's no more,
    And magnify his reign?
Sure never mortal man before
    Would have his grief again.

Farewell the long-continued ache,
The days a-dream, the nights awake,
I will rejoice and merry make,
    And never more complain.

King Love is dead and gone for aye,
    Who ruled with might and main,
For with a bitter word one day,
    I found my tyrant slain,
And he in Heathenesse was bred,
Nor ever was baptized, 'tis said,
Nor is of any creed, and dead
    Can never rise again.

RETROSPECT

Here beside my Paris fire, I sit alone and ponder
All my life of long ago that lies so far asunder;
"Here, how came I thence?" I say, and greater
    grows the wonder
As I recall the farms and fields and placid hamlets
    yonder.

... See, the meadow-sweet is white against the water-courses,
Marshy lands are kingcup-gay and bright with streams and sources,
Dew-bespangled shines the hill where half-abloom the gorse is;
And all the northern fallows steam beneath the ploughing horses.

There's the red-brick-chimneyed house, the ivied haunt of swallows,
All its garden up and down and full of hills and hollows;
Past the lawn, the sunken fence whose brink the laurel follows;
And then the knee-deep pasture where the herd for ever wallows!

So they've clipped the lilac bush: a thousand thousand pities!
'Twas the blue old-fashioned sort that never grows in cities.
There we little children played and chaunted aimless ditties,
While oft the old grandsire looked at us and smiled his Nunc Dimittis!

Green, O green with ancient peace, and full of sap and
    sunny,
Lusty fields of Warwickshire, O land of milk and
    honey,
Might I live to pluck again a spike of agrimony,
A silver tormentilla leaf or ladysmock upon ye!

Patience, for I keep at heart your pure and perfect
    seeming,
I can see you wide awake as clearly as in dreaming,
Softer, with an inner light, and dearer, to my deeming,
Than when beside your brooks at noon I watched the
    sallows gleaming!

TWILIGHT

When I was young the twilight seemed too long.

How often on the western window-seat
  I leaned my book against the misty pane
  And spelled the last enchanting lines again,
The while my mother hummed an ancient song,
Or sighed a little and said: "The hour is sweet!"
When I, rebellious, clamoured for the light.

But now I love the soft approach of night,
   And now with folded hands I sit and dream
   While all too fleet the hours of twilight seem ;
And thus I know that I am growing old.

O granaries of Age! O manifold
And royal harvest of the common years!
There are in all thy treasure-house no ways
But lead by soft descent and gradual slope
To memories more exquisite than Hope.
Thine is the Iris born of olden tears,
And thrice more happy are the happy days
That live divinely in thy lingering rays.[i]
So autumn roses bear a lovelier flower;
So in the emerald after-sunset hour
The orchard wall and trembling aspen-trees
Appear an infinite Hesperides.
Ay, as at dusk we sit with folded hands,
Who knows, who cares in what enchanted lands
We wander while the undying memories throng?

When I was young the twilight seemed too long.

ROBERT, LORD HOUGHTON
Born 1858

A WET SUNSET IN SOUTH AFRICA

Across the waste of dreary veldt,
   Unmarked by hut, or knoll, or hollow,
The lifeless mountain's arid belt
   Trends southward, far as eye can follow.

A fitful rain is dripping still,
   Close to the plain the swifts are skimming;
The thirsty soil has drunk its fill,
   And left a thousand pools a-brimming.

The west is rapt from sight and sense,
   Lost in a haze of fairy yellow;
A sadness, born we know not whence,
   Falls with that light divinely mellow:

Where hangs unseen the guiding Cross,
   The lightning's magic veil is lifting,
Clouds like Atlantic billows toss,
   From summit on to summit drifting;

Eastward, a cold unearthly sheen
   Of mists fantastically riven,
All steel and silver damascene,
   Bright armour for the hosts of heaven.

Unbidden memories of home
   The stranger landscape seem to hallow,—
The tender touch of English Crome
   On Norfolk broad, and stream, and shallow,—

A dream of looming towers that crown
   A northern city's smoke and shadow,
Where Lincoln Church looks stately down
   On flooded fen and steaming meadow.

One moment,—off the vanished sun
   A redder fire of glory flushes,
The pools grow rosy one by one,
   The pallid east in answer blushes;

Another,—half the glow is gone,
   The near and far in shade are blended,
Black-plumaged night flies swiftly on,
   The curtain falls,—the dream is ended.

A QUESTION

*"Methinks too little cost
For a moment so found, so lost!"*

Ought the Man to be cut,
  Just as much as the Lady?
When they've met Justice Butt
Ought the Man to be cut?
When they've stuck in a rut
  Down a lane that is shady;—
Ought the Man to be cut,
  Just as much as the Lady?

NORMAN GALE

Born 1862

A BIRD IN THE HAND

Look at this ball of intractable fluff,
   Panting and staring with piteous eyes!
What a rebellion of heart! what a ruff
   Tickles my hand as the missel-thrush tries,
Pecking my hand with her termagant bill,
   How to escape (and I love her, the sweet!)
Back where the clustering oaks on the hill
   Climb to the blue with their branches, and meet!

Nay, polished beak, you are pecking a friend!
   Bird of the grassland, you bleed at the wing!
Stay with me, love; in captivity mend
   Wrong that was wrought by the boy and his sling.
Oh for a Priest of the Birds to arise,
   Wonderful words on his lips that persuade
Reasoning creatures to leave to the skies
   Song at its purest a-throb in the glade!

Bow, woodland heart, to the yoke for a while!
   Soon shall the lyrics of wind in the trees
Stir you to pipe in the green forest-aisle,
   God send me there with the grass to my knees!
See, I am stroking my cheek with thy breast,
   Ah, how the bountiful velvet is fair!
Stay with me here for your healing and rest,
   Stay, for I love you, delight of the air!

KATHARINE TYNAN

Born 1862

GOLDEN LILIES

O Daffodils all aflame
I know from whence ye came
To warm March with your blaze!
   As Gabriel went a-winging
Through flowering country ways
   He heard your trumpets ringing.

God's Paradise this was,
With a city of rainbow glass,
The River of Life there flows,
   The Tree of Life there blooming
Hath many a name that glows
   Like flower and fruit illuming.

But Gabriel going down,
With a gold gown and crown,
Was grave as him bestead;
   Great tidings he was bringing,

To raise the earth from dead,
    And set the heaven to singing.

"Oh, young," he said, " is she,
God's Maid and Queen, Marie;"
He said, "I will bring down
    These golden trumpets blowing,
And lay them on her gown,
    To glad her with their showing."

Queen Marie in her bower
Had a white lily in flower,
And Gabriel brought the gold,
    The gold lily that ever
Blowing his trumpet bold,
    Declares her praise for ever.

A TIRED HEART

Dear Lord! if one should some day come to Thee,
  Weary exceedingly, and poor, and worn,
  With bleeding feet sore-pierced of many a thorn
And lips athirst, and eyes too tired to see,
  And, falling down before Thy face, should say:
  "Lord, my day counts but as an idle day,

My hands have garnered fruit of no fair tree,
   Empty am I of stores of oil and corn,
   Broken am I and utterly forlorn,
Yet in Thy vineyard hast Thou room for me?"
        Wouldst turn Thy face away?
Nay, Thou wouldst lift Thy lost sheep tenderly.

"Lord! Thou art pale, as one that travaileth,
   And Thy wounds bleed where feet and hands were
      riven;
Thou hast lain all these years, in balms of Heaven,
Since Thou wert broken in the arms of Death,
   And these have healed not!" "Child! be comforted.
   I trod the winepress where thy feet have bled;
Yea, on the Cross, I cried with mighty breath,
   Thirsting for thee, whose love was elsewhere given,
   I, God, have followed thee from dawn to even,
With yearning heart, by many a moor and heath,
        My sheep that wanderèd!
Now on My breast, Mine arm its head beneath."

Then, if this stricken one cried out to Thee,
   "Now mine eyes see that Thou art passing fair,
   And Thy face marred of men beyond compare,"
And so should fall to weeping bitterly,
   With, "Lord, I longed for other love than Thine,
   And my feet followed earthly lovers fine,

Turning from where Thy gaze entreated me;
   Now these grow cold, and wander otherwhere,
   And I, heart-empty, poor, and sick, and bare,
Loved of no lover, turn at last to Thee;"—
        Wouldst stretch Thine hands divine,
And stroke the bowed head very pityingly?

"Will not My love suffice, though great thy pain?"
   "Ah, Lord! all night without a lighted house,
   While some within held revel and carouse,
My lost heart wandered in the wind and rain,
   And moaned unheard amid the tempest's din."
   "Peace, peace! if one had oped to let thee in,
Perchance this hour were lost for that hour's gain;
   Wouldst thou have sought Me then, with thy new vows?
Ah, child! I too, with bleeding feet and brows,
Knocked all the night at a heart's door in vain,
        And saw the dawn begin,
On My gold head the dews have left a stain."

HERBERT P. HORNE

Born 1864

AMICO SUO

When on my country walks I go,
   I never am alone:
Though, whom 'twere pleasure then to know,
   Are gone, and you are gone;
From every side discourses flow.

There are rich counsels in the trees,
   And converse in the air;
All magic thoughts in those and these
   And what is sweet and rare;
And everything that living is.

But most I love the meaner sort,
   For they have voices too;
Yet speak with tongues that never hurt,
   As ours are apt to do:
The weeds, the grass, the common wort.

ARTHUR SYMONS
Born 1865

RAIN ON THE DOWN

Night, and the down by the sea,
   And the veil of rain on the down;
And she came through the mist and the rain to me
   From the safe warm lights of the town.

The rain shone in her hair,
   And her face gleamed in the rain;
And only the night and the rain were there
   As she came to me out of the rain.

EMMY

Emmy's exquisite youth and her virginal air,
   Eyes and teeth in the flash of a musical smile,
Come to me out of the past, and I see her there
   As I saw her once for a while.

Emmy's laughter rings in my ears, as bright,
  Fresh and sweet as the voice of a mountain brook,
And still I hear her telling us tales that night,
  Out of Boccaccio's book.

There, in the midst of the villainous dancing-hall,
  Leaning across the table, over the beer,
While the music maddened the whirling skirts of the ball,
  As the midnight hour drew near,

There with the women, haggard, painted and old,
  One fresh bud in a garland withered and stale,
She, with her innocent voice and her clear eyes, told
  Tale after shameless tale;

And ever the witching smile, to her face beguiled,
  Paused and broadened, and broke in a ripple of fun,
And the soul of a child looked out of the eyes of a child,
  Or ever the tale was done.

O my child, who wronged you first, and began
  First the dance of death that you dance so well?
Soul for soul: and I think the soul of a man
  Shall answer for yours in hell.

RUDYARD KIPLING

Born 1865

MANDALAY

By the old Moulmein Pagoda, looking eastward to the sea,
There's a Burma girl a-settin', an' I know she thinks o' me;
For the wind is in the palm-trees, an' the temple-bells they say:
"Come you back, you British soldier; come you back to Mandalay!"
    Come you back to Mandalay,
    Where the old Flotilla lay:
    Can't you 'ear their paddles chunkin' from Rangoon to Mandalay?
    O the road to Mandalay,
    Where the flyin' fishes play,
    An' the dawn comes up like thunder outer China 'crost the Bay!

'Er petticut was yaller an' 'er little cap was green,
An' 'er name was Supi-yaw-lat—jes the same as Theebaw's Queen,
An' I seed her fust a-smoking of a whackin' white cheroot,
An' a-wastin' Christian kisses on an' 'eathen idol's foot:
    Bloomin' idol made o' mud—
    Wot they called the Great Gawd Budd—
    Plucky lot she cared for idols when I kissed 'er where she stud!
    On the road to Mandalay,—

When the mist was on the rice-fields an' the sun was droppin' slow,
She'd git 'er little banjo an' she'd sing "*Kulla-lo-lo!*"
With 'er arm upon my shoulder an' her cheek agin my cheek
We useter watch the steamers an' the *hathis* pilin' teak.
    Elephints a-pilin' teak
    In the sludgy, squdgy creek,
    Where the silence 'ung that 'eavy you was 'arf afraid to speak!
    On the road to Mandalay,—

But that's all shove be'ind me—long ago an' fur away,
An' there ain't no 'buses runnin' from the Bank to Mandalay;

An' I'm learnin' 'ere in London what the ten-year
    sodger tells :
" If you've 'eard the East a'callin', why, you won't 'eed
    nothin' else."
        No ! you won't 'eed nothin' else
        But them spicy garlic smells
        An' the sunshine an' the palm-trees an' the
            tinkly temple-bells !
        On the road to Mandalay,—

I am sick o' wastin' leather on these gutty pavin'-stones,
An' the blasted Henglish drizzle wakes the fever in
    my bones ;
Tho' I walks with fifty 'ousemaids outer Chelsea to the
    Strand,
An' they talks a lot o' lovin', but wot do they under-
    stand ?
        Beefy face an' grubby 'and—
        Law ! wot *do* they understand ?
        I've a neater, sweeter maiden in a cleaner,
            greener land !
        On the road to Mandalay,—

Ship me somewheres east of Suez where the best is
    like the worst,
Where there aren't no Ten Commandments, an' a man
    can raise a thirst ;

For the Temple-bells are callin', an' it's there that I would be—
By the old Moulmein Pagoda, lookin' lazy at the sea—
    On the road to Mandalay,
    Where the old Flotilla lay,
    With our sick beneath the awnings when we went to Mandalay!
    Oh, the road to Mandalay,
    Where the flyin' fishes play,
    An' the dawn comes up like thunder outer China 'crost the Bay!

L'ENVOI

There's a whisper down the field where the year has shot her yield,
  And the ricks stand grey to the sun,
Singing :—" Over then, come over, for the bee has quit the clover,
  And your English summer's done."
    You have heard the beat of the off-shore wind,
    And the thresh of the deep-sea rain ;
    You have heard the song—how long! how long?
    Pull out on the trail again!

Ha' done with the Tents of Shem, dear lass,
We've seen the seasons through,
And it's time to turn on the old trail, our own
    trail, the out trail,
Pull out, pull out, on the Long Trail—the trail
    that is always new.

It's North you may run to the rime-ringed sun
  Or South to the blind Horn's hate;
Or East all the way into Mississippi Bay,
  Or West to the Golden Gate;
    Where the blindest bluffs hold good, dear lass,
    And the wildest tales are true,
    And the men bulk big on the old trail, our own
        trail, the out trail,
    And life runs large on the Long Trail—the trail
        that is always new.

The days are sick and cold, and the skies are grey
    and old,
  And the twice-breathed airs blow damp;
And I'd sell my tired soul for the bucking beam-sea
    roll
  Of a black Bilbao tramp;
    With her load-line over her hatch, dear lass,
    And a drunken Dago crew,

T

  And her nose held down on the old trail, our own
    trail, the out trail,
  From Cadiz Bar on the Long Trail—the trail that
    is always new.

There be triple ways to take, of the eagle or the snake,
  Or the way of a man with a maid;
But the sweetest way to me is a ship's upon the sea
  In the heel of the North-East Trade;
    Can you hear the crash on her bows, dear lass,
    And the drum of the racing screw,
    As she slips it green on the old trail, our own trail,
      the out trail,
    As she lifts and 'scends on the Long Trail—the
      trail that is always new?

See the shaking funnels roar, with the Peter at the fore,
  And the fenders grind and heave,
And the derricks clack and grate, as the tackle hooks
    the crate,
  And the fall-rope whines through the sheave;
    It's "Gang-plank up and in," dear lass,
    It's "Hawsers warp her through!"
    And it's "All clear aft" on the old trail, our own
      trail, the out trail,
    We're backing down on the Long Trail—the trail
      that is always new.

O the mutter overside, when the port-fog holds us tied,
  And the sirens hoot their dread!
When foot by foot we creep o'er the hueless viewless deep
  To the sob of the questing lead!
    It's down by the Lower Hope, dear lass,
    With the Gunfleet Sands in view,
      Till the Mouse swings green on the old trail, our own trail, the out trail,
      And the Gull Light lifts on the Long Trail—the trail that is always new.

O the blazing tropic night, when the wake's a welt of light
  That holds the hot sky tame,
And the steady fore-foot snores through the planet-powdered floors
  Where the scared whale flukes in flame!
    Her plates are scarred by the sun, dear lass,
    And her ropes are taunt with the dew,
      For we're booming down on the old trail, our own trail, the out trail,
      We're sagging south on the Long Trail—the trail that is always new.

Then home, get her home, where the drunken rollers comb,
  And the shouting seas drive by,

And the engines stamp and ring, and the wet bows
　　reel and swing,
　And the Southern Cross rides high!
　　Yes, the old lost stars wheel back, dear lass,
　　That blaze in the velvet blue.
　　They're all old friends on the old trail, our own
　　　　trail, the out trail,
　　They're God's own guides on the Long Trail—the
　　　　trail that is always new.

Fly forward, O my heart, from the Foreland to the
　　Start—
　We're steaming all-too slow,
And it's twenty thousand mile to our little lazy isle
　Where the trumpet-orchids blow!
　　You have heard the call of the off-shore wind
　　And the voice of the deep-sea rain;
　　You have heard the song—how long, how long?
　　Pull out on the trail again!

　　The Lord knows what we may find, dear lass,
　　And the Deuce knows what we may do—
　　But we're back once more on the old trail, our
　　　　own trail, the out trail,
　　We're down, hull down on the Long Trail—the
　　　　trail that is always new.

RICHARD LE GALLIENNE

Born 1866

THE WONDER-CHILD

"Our little babe," each said, "shall be
Like unto thee"—"Like unto *thee!*"
   "Her mother's"—"Nay, his father's"—"eyes,"
   "Dear curls like thine"—but each replies,
"As thine, all thine, and naught of me."

What sweet solemnity to see
The little life upon thy knee,
   And whisper as so soft it lies,—
      "Our little babe!"

For, whether it be he or she,
A David or a Dorothy,
   "As mother fair," or "father wise,"
   Both when it's "good," and when it cries,
One thing is certain,—it will be
      Our little babe.

AUTUMN

The year grows still again, the surging wake
  Of full-sailed summer folds its furrows up
    As after passing of an argosy
    Old silence settles back upon the sea,
  And ocean grows as placid as a cup.
    Spring, the young morn, and Summer, the strong noon,
Have dreamed and done and died for Autumn's sake:
  Autumn that finds not for a loss so dear
    Solace in stack and garner hers too soon—
Autumn, the faithful widow of the year.

Autumn, a poet once so full of song,
  Wise in all rhymes of blossom and of bud,
Hath lost the early magic of his tongue,
  And hath no passion in his failing blood.
Hear ye no sound of sobbing in the air?
  'Tis his. Low bending in a secret lane,
Late blooms of second childhood in his hair,
  He tries old magic, like a dotard mage;
    Tries spell and spell, to weep and try again:
Yet not a daisy bears, and everywhere
    The hedgerow rattles like an empty cage.

He hath no pleasure in his silken skies,
    Nor delicate ardours of the yellow land;
Yea, dead, for all its gold, the woodland lies,
    And all the throats of music filled with sand.
Neither to him across the stubble field
    May stack nor garner any comfort bring,
        Who loveth more this jasmine he hath made,
The little tender rhyme he yet can sing,
Than yesterday, with all its pompous yield,
    Or all its shaken laurels on his head.

ALL SUNG

What shall I sing when all is sung,
    And every tale is told,
And in the world is nothing young
    That was not long since old?

Why should I fret unwilling ears
    With old things sung anew,
While voices from the old dead years
    Still go on singing too?

A dead man singing of his maid
    Makes all my rhymes in vain,

Yet his poor lips must fade and fade,
  And mine shall kiss again.

Why should I strive through weary moons
  To make my music true?
Only the dead men know the tunes
  The live world dances to.

INDEX OF FIRST LINES.

	PAGE
Across the waste of dreary veldt	257
A little marsh-plant, yellow green	146
All day long and every day	87
All night as in my dreams I lay	16
All travail of high thought	74
A naked house, a naked moor	242
And now I speak, not with the bird's free voice	198
And shall I weep that Love's no more	252
And why say ye that I must leave	126
An idle poet, here and there	33
Assemble, all ye maidens, at the door	222
Atlantid islands, phantom-fair	217
Back to the flower-town, side by side	141
Beating Heart! we come again	27
Behold the Court of Penance. Four gaunt walls	165
Beneath the sand-storm John the Pilgrim prays	137
Between two golden tufts of summer grass	231
Brave as a falcon and as merciless	162
But on another day the King said, Come	59
By the old Moulmein Pagoda, looking eastward to the sea	269
Day of my life! Where can she get	189
Dear Lord! if one should some day come to Thee	263
Does the road wind up-hill all the way	46
Emmy's exquisite youth and her virginal air	267

INDEX OF FIRST LINES

	PAGE
Fair now is the spring-tide, now earth lies beholding	107
Far off the old snows ever new	220
Flower of the medlar	248
God said, " Bring little children unto me "	6
Good pastry is vended	28
Had she come all the way for this	92
Hail ! once again, that sweet strong note	118
He lived in that past Georgian day	173
He lives within the hollow wood	237
Here beside my Paris fire, I sit alone and ponder	253
Here I'd come when weariest	229
Here, in this leafy place	185
How strange a thing a lover seems	31
How sweet the harmonies of Afternoon	1
I do not bid thee spare me, O dreadful mother	152
I dream'd I was in Sicily	249
I drew it from its china tomb	167
If I forget	239
If I have faltered more or less	243
If I should die this night, (as well might be	195
If love is not worth loving, then life is not worth living	57
If only in dreams may Man be fully blest	138
I found him openly wearing her token	241
If those who wield the Rod forget	181
I have loved flowers that fade	225
I heard the voice of my own true love	112
I know a little garden close	102
In a coign of the cliff between lowland and highland	158
In after days when grasses high	194
In ruling well what guerdon? Life runs low	135

INDEX OF FIRST LINES

	PAGE
I saw you toss the kites on high	244
It was not like your great and gracious ways	35
I watch you through the garden walks	179
King Philip had vaunted his claims	192
Latest, earliest of the year	120
Let me at last be laid	66
Lilac and gold and green	163
Look at this ball of intractable fluff	260
Love is enough: ho ye who seek saving	105
Lycius! the female race is all the same	19
Men deemed thee fallen, did they? fallen like Rome	125
Methought I met a Lady yestereven	39
Mortals who attempt the seas	210
My little Son, who look'd from thoughtful eyes	34
My love whose heart is tender said to me	55
My only Love is always near	26
Night, and the down by the sea	267
Now did you mark a falcon	48
Now Neptune, joyful of the sacrifice	99
O Daffodils all aflame	262
Of all the downfalls in the world	57
Of Heaven or Hell I have no power to sing	103
Of Mary's pains may now learn whoso will	84
Oh for the young heart like a fountain playing	24
Once Cagn was like a father, kind and good	230
O so drowsy! In a daze	203
Ought the Man to be cut	259
Our little babe, each said, shall be	277

INDEX OF FIRST LINES

	PAGE
Out in the meadows the young grass springs	234
O where are you going with your love-locks flowing	44
Pale, beyond porch and portal	144
Play then and sing; we too have played	148
Say not of me that weakly I declined	245
See, where a fireship in mid ocean blazes	216
Sing clearlier, Muse, or evermore be still	246
Spirit of Trajan! What a world is here	163
Sunrise! and it is summer, and the morning	200
Sweet singer of the Spring, when the new world	80
The curtains were half drawn, the floor was swept	54
The feathers of the willow	83
The forest rears on lifted arms	9
The hours are passing slow	227
The ladies of St. James's	186
The Lady of the Hills with crimes untold	136
There needs not choral song, nor organs pealing	22
There's a whisper down the field where the year has shot her yield	272
There's one great bunch of stars in heaven	247
There, where the sun shines first	37
The Rose in the garden slipped her bud	184
The silent Forces of the World	71
The sunrise wakes the lark to sing	48
The tree many-rooted	155
The year grows still again, the surging wake	278
This the house of Circe, queen of charms	132
This was the matter of the note	170
Tiny slippers of gold and green	61
To the forgotten dead	250

INDEX OF FIRST LINES

	PAGE
What shall I sing when all is sung	279
We wish to declare how the Birds of the air all high Institutions designed	213
When I am dead, my dearest	47
When I was dead, my spirit turned	51
When I was young, I said to Sorrow	15
When I was young the twilight seemed too long	255
When on my country walks I go	266
When Spring comes laughing	178
When the hounds of spring are on winter's traces	139
Where shall I find a white rose blowing	55
Where sunless rivers weep	52
Why should we seek at all to gain	69
With forces well-nigh spent	75
You hail from Dream-land, Dragon-fly?	251